2012
THE BEST WOMEN'S STAGE
MONOLOGUES AND SCENES

2012
THE BEST WOMEN'S STAGE MONOLOGUES AND SCENES

Edited and with a Foreword
by Lawrence Harbison

MONOLOGUE AUDITION SERIES

Smith and Kraus Publishers

ISBN: 1575257904
ISBN: 9781575257907
Library of Congress Control Number: 2164-2362

Typesetting and layout:Elizabeth E. Monteleone
Cover Design: Elizabeth E. Monteleone

A Smith and Kraus book
177 Lyme Road, Hanover, NH 03755
Editorial 603.643.6431 To Order 1.800.558.2846
www.smithandkraus.com

Printed in the United States of America

CONTENTS

MONOLOGUES

SCENES

FOREWORD

Here you will find a rich and varied selection of monologues and scenes for women from plays which were produced and/or published in the 2011-2012 theatrical season. Most are for younger performers (teens through thirties) but there are also some excellent pieces for older women as well. Some are comic (laughs), some are dramatic (generally, no laughs). Some are rather short, some are rather long. All represent the best in contemporary playwriting.

Several of the monologues are by playwrights whose work may be familiar to you, such as Don Nigro, Stephen Adly Guirgis, David Lindsay-Abaire, Adam Rapp, Carson Kreitzer, José Rivera and Itamar Moses; others are by exciting up-and-comers such as Molly Smith Metzler, Jessica Dickey, Chad Beckim, Clinton A. Johnson, Lydia R. Diamond and Katori Hall. The scenes are by veterans such as Don Nigro, Wendy MacLeod, and Saviana Stanescu, and exciting new writers such as Merridith Allen, Stephen Bittrich, Jacqueline Goldfinger and C.S. Hanson. All are representative of the best contemporary writing for the stage.

Most of the plays from which these monologues have been culled have been published and, hence, are readily available either from the publisher/licensor or from a theatrical book store such as the Drama Book Shop in New York. A few plays may not be published for a while, in which case contact the author or his agent to request a copy of the entire text of the play which contains the monologue or scene which suits your fancy. Information on publishers/rights holders may be found in the Rights & Permissions section in the back of this anthology.

Break a leg in that audition! Knock 'em dead in class!

Lawrence Harbison
Brooklyn, NY

MONOLOGUES

4000 MILES

Amy Herzog

Seriocomic
Vera, ninety-one

Vera, is speaking to Bec, her grandson's on-again-off-again girlfriend. While the two women wait for Leo (who is late), Vera tries to impart her light-hearted perspective about men's occasional slip-ups and infidelities to the clearly perturbed younger woman.

VERA: When I was first married. Not to Joe, to my first husband, Arthur. It was a week or two we had been married and a woman showed up at our apartment with luggage. Arthur said to me, oh I forgot to tell you, before we were married I promised I would take her away for the weekend and I didn't want to fink on a promise.
(laughing)
So I said all right, and they went away, and I left my key on the piano and went home to my parents. He came to my parents at the end of the weekend begging and pleading and I thought it was funny that he had been so stupid so I went home with him. It wasn't the last time he cheated. When we had been married six months he went out to Hollywood with a woman . . . oh god, what was her name. She was rich, and neurotic. Muriel. He and Muriel went out there to write a screenplay and her father bankrolled them and Arthur never sent me a penny. And I guess they were having an affair because when he tried to end it she threatened to kill herself, and that was a terrible mess. One time we were all at Café Society . . . And she followed me into a cab and said, can't we be friends? It eats away at me that you're angry at me and so forth. And I said listen, Muriel, there are people you like and people you don't, and I don't like you, and I want you out of this cab. And she cried and carried on, this woman who had been sleeping with my husband for two years . . .
(long pause.)

Then there was the waitress he met in Arkansas. And he came home and confessed he was in love with her, and I said listen, she's a hick, you have nothing in common, I'm sure the sex is terrific and whatnot but why don't you go back there and spend a few weeks with her and see if there's really enough there for you to leave our marriage. And he did. And sure enough he came back and said you're right, we ran out of things to talk about. And that was that. He was a cheater and a drunk, but I liked him till the day he died.

ABOUT SPONTANEOUS COMBUSTION

Sherry Kramer

Seriocomic
Mary Catherine, late twenties-early thirties

> *Mary Catherine hasn't been home in a long time—she considers herself a bit too sophisticated to fit in with her all American, quirky but wholesome family. She's come back for the funeral of her ancient Aunt Emily, who died from the shock of seeing Amalia, Mary Catherine's younger sister, having sex on a pile of clothing with her boyfriend. Now Amalia refuses to get out of the bathtub—she believes that spontaneous combustion is what killed her aunt and what will kill her, and the only way to stay safe is to stay in the water. Mary Catherine is not convinced. She's pretty sure you can't make a life in a bathtub, and even if you could—you still wouldn't be safe. She decides it's her mission to get Amalia out of the tub, and goes into the bathroom to confront her.*

MARY CATHERINE: Molly, when people spend days sitting in bathtubs of cold water they catch cold. Yeah, yeah, I know you're not afraid of catching cold. You're afraid of catching hot. But basically, Molly, I believe it all comes down to a fear of catching a temperature other than your own. This is why, I freely admit, your decision to silently semi-drown yourself makes no sense to me. If it is even possible to separate hot and cold, ying and yang, if it is even possible, spiritually, theoretically you still can't do it in this instance, because getting a fever is the very body to the soul of catching cold. This spontaneous combustion is just a screen, Molly, It's not what really has you scared. No. What you, Amalia Parker, are frightened of, what has you up to your neck in the wet quarter-nelson of fear is nothing more, nothing less, nothing but the common cold. For most women I know, a man represents a cure for a vital, everyday illness. But they can never quite remember whether the rule really is feed a fever and starve a cold. It sounds obviously onomatopoeic. And the instinct once thwarted, they end up starving the wrong mouth for the greater part of their lives. They get so busy pushing men into places inside them that are not connected to even the suggestion of a digestive tract. Well, maybe you're right. Maybe discretion is the better part of valor. If you can't say something nice, don't say anything at all, and all. You know, when we were kids I thought it said, "the better part of velour." "Discretion is the better part of velour." Ever since then I've always suspected that discretion was somehow synthetic. Counterfeit. That's what I think now, Molly.

(Pause)

Molly, it's just not all that attractive, you're sitting there all wet, not saying anything. I mean, your little mermaid routine, I can go for that. But I keep wanting to ask you if the cat's got your tongue. Tuna fish, Molly. That's what this charade suggests to me. Tuna fish. And I don't get it.

Information on this playwright may be found at www.smithandkraus.com. Click on the AUTHORS tab.

An Accident

Lydia Stryk

Dramatic
Libby, late twenties-early forties

An Accident is set in a hospital room where Libby lies in a bed. She is a strong-willed, dynamic and funny woman in a moment of terrible crisis. She has lost much of her memory and is able to move only her head at this point in the play, though she has a more hopeful prognosis. Anton, the man who ran her over in a supermarket parking lot, has chosen to visit her on a regular basis, enduring her anger and his own guilt. In this monologue, Libby responds to Anton's attempt to make her see herself as a survivor, someone special.

LIBBY: And those who don't survive? What about them? That miracle window washer who fell 47 stories? He was walking his dog six months later! But look at his poor brother. The unlucky window-washer. No miracle for him. And it was the wind that saved the one, not some fucking miracle. Or it's the wind that's the miracle. A bowel movement is a miracle. From where I'm laying. And his survival does not make him a hero, okay? But his life might, but who cares about that? Illegal immigrant. Well, he certainly gave back-breaking work a new meaning! All I'm saying is. I was lucky. I admit it. But it doesn't make me special. And it didn't have to be like that. Don't take comfort in that. I could be dead. Or a vegetable, is that what they call it? And why do they call it that? A vegetable. It's demeaning. Who dared to come up with that?
(She lets out a sigh.)
I should have just died and done with it. I'm not grateful, Anton. To have survived. I am not grateful, you hear me? To be alive. I don't feel like starting over with a new lease on life. Besides, everyone loves an untimely death. You ever notice that? And there's nothing we love better than a tragic accident. That cosmic fate. That mother of all bad

luck. We can't get enough of it. Preferably, you're taken in your prime, the more beautiful the better. A princess, a sports hero, an actress. It's so riveting. So damn unfathomable. It's so cathartic. So ancient Greek. So primal. But survival? The damaged goods? We're embarrassed by it. Tongue-tied. I know you're tongue-tied, Anton. I see you struggling. Cheer up. I'd trade places with you any day. If it makes you feel any better. I'd rather have hit you. Than be like this. I'd rather have killed you. Than this. I hope that's a comfort.

*Information on this playwright may be found at
www.smithandkraus.com. Click on the AUTHORS tab.*

ADORATION OF THE OLD WOMAN

José Rivera

Dramatic
Adoración, twenties.

Adoración, a ghost, is talking to Dona Belen. While she was alive, Adoración had an affair with Belen's husband Toli. Now that she's dead, Adoración haunts Belen's bed at night by telling Belen how much she loved her husband Toli.

ADORACIÓN: Don Toli wasn't the strongest man in Las Arenas. But you never measure a man's true strength by the amount of suffering he can take or the amount of cane he can cut in a day or how many shots of rum it takes to make him smile after a day of hard labor. When I took water to the men in the fields, or filled my *fiambrera* with hot *asopao*, I treated each man like he was a king. I knew work was scarce and soon the *tiempo muerto* would come and the *guajana* would cover the fields and there would be no work for nine months and much suffering. Yes, women whispered that I was a whore because I went to those fields to refresh the men with water and soup, even though I had no husband, or *novio*, and a girl my age was never allowed alone in those fields with all those men. But I didn't care about the rumors and dirty words! Those men were heroes in my eyes, each one, not mules like the foremen thought. Each man was a soldier fighting against the starvation that always seemed only a day or two away. It shocked me that every woman in Las Arenas wasn't out there with me. The nerve of those bitches calling me whore! *(beat)* The first time I gave Don Toli his water, I knew. How a man can work under the hot sun, bent like an animal and still have the willpower for sexy thoughts is beyond me. He took my water. And, later, he took the rest of me without lifting a finger. Sometimes you come face to face with your definition of manhood. Not your mother's, not your religion's, not your barrio's. Yours. And I did.

Adoration of the Old Woman

José Rivera

Dramatic
Adoración, twenties.

*Adoración is a ghost. She's speaking to her granddaughter
Vanessa. Vanessa doesn't know that Adoración is her grandmother. In this monologue Adoración explains how she gave
birth to Vanessa's mother and how the baby was taken from
her after her death.*

ADORACIÓN: The old lady, she lied to you. Yes, I slept with
Don Toli and everyone in Las Arenas knew—including
Doña Belen. But no one dared say a word. Then I got
pregnant. And that changed everything. He stopped wanting
me—completely. I was so desperate, one day I went to church
to look for him. He was there—next to Belen. She looked at
my growing belly, her mouth opened for one word: whore.
Over and over—in front of God, Mary, the entire town. Soon
I was known at the Mulatta Whore of Las Arenas. When
Don Toli started saying it too—the words were like knives
right into my body! My baby was born . . . and the dirty
words of Las Arenas killed me. The day I was buried, Don
Toli came to my house and my mother gave him my baby.
And he took my baby to Belen and said, "This is our baby
now. Celia is our baby." Belen said yes. And took her in.
And never told you that your grandmother Celia was my
baby. Vanessa—you my baby. Ay! It was what the old witch
wanted more than anything, to make life, to see it coming
out from between her legs, complete, breathing, hearing it
laugh, its little fingers scrambling up to touch her. She never
had that. All her stillborn hopes are buried under a Ceiba
tree in Las Arenas. Each branch of the tree is another dead
hope. My one baby—my girl—walked away from all that
death. To think, to pray—and maybe, somehow, if there's
justice, to remember the passage from my body into the
humid air. To remember the liquid I surrounded her with,

the thunder of my heart, the salt sea-water of my blood. I told you to live and you did . . .

After

Chad Beckim

Comic
Susie, early thirties

Susie shares a revelation about drug store practices with Monty, a customer she's just met.

SUSIE: Know what I just realized? Deodorant should actually be in this aisle, not two aisles down. Deodorant helps you smell good, right? And toothpaste helps your breath smell good, right? Wouldn't it make more sense for them to all be in the same aisle? Huh. That's really cool. You're not one of those "Axe" guys, are you? You know—
(She "sprays" herself.)
pssssssshhhhhhhhhhtttttttt!
You've never seen it? "Axe"? It's this horribly smelly shit that for some reason guys think smell good and spray all over themselves. You don't look like an "Axe" guy. Please don't be an "Axe" guy. I don't get that, you know? Like, you'll see these good looking guys, well groomed, well maintained, together, the kind of guy that you see and secretly think, "He looks like a nice guy to talk to," only then they walk past you and they smell like they just got stuck in a cologne thunderstorm. You're Latino, right? And you don't stink like that. You smell natural. Like soap or something. Which is good. So what's up with that? I only ask because, it actually made me stop dating black and Latin guys. Which sucks, because I actually prefer black and Latin guys. White guys are too boring and Asian guys have mom issues. And Jews.
(She hangs her head again.)
I'm sorry. That wasn't racist, was it? I'm sorry. I'm not a racist, I swear. My ex is Latino.
(A short beat. She smiles nervously.)
I'm sorry. I talk too much. I say too much dumb stuff. And I'm sorry I forced that toothbrush on you. I'm working on

it, but it's . . . The deodorant aisle is that way. *(She points.)* Two aisles down.

Al's Business Cards

Josh Koenigsberg

Dramatic
Eileen Lee, late twenties to mid-forties

Eileen, a real estate agent and recovering alcoholic, is out to dinner with prospective client Al Gurvis, who has asked her what it was that made her quit drinking.

EILEEN: (chuckling self-consciously) You mean was there a specific incident that made me hit bottom and try to 'fight my way back up'? Um, yeah, actually, sort of. I, um,
(She laughs at herself.)
God, this is so stupid. I basically—I uh,
(She takes a deep breath.)
I woke my mom's cat up from a nap. Well it just . . . it started this whole chain reaction, y'know? I mean basically what happened is, two years ago, right before I got sober, I went home for Thanksgiving. And the night I arrived, first thing I did is I went straight to the local bar and started drinking really heavily. I mean, one—it was my birthday, cause my birthday was on Thanksgiving that year, and I was really depressed. And two—it was ladies night, buy one get one free—so that right there just, like, doubled the incentive to get wasted. So I just drank and drank til it got to the point where you close your eyes and it feels like you're on a re-ally wobbly carousel? Anyway, I woke up the next morning, and I had to pee so badly. And I didn't think I was gonna make it to the bathroom at the end of the hall. So instead, I just went into my mom's room next door and used her bathroom. But when I got out, I saw the cat was taking a nap on my mom's bed—and he looked so cute y'know?—so naturally, I just started petting it. But apparently he didn't want me to pet him—because what he did is he got up and he ran away from me—he ran downstairs where the other place he liked to sleep was, right behind the kitchen sink. But downstairs my mom was cooking, making this special

dish or something, and she had my grandmother's price-less antique bowl out, and when my cat jumped up onto the kitchen counter to get to his other resting place, he of course knocked over my grandmother's priceless antique bowl, causing it to shatter everywhere, which in turn caused my mom to start yelling and cursing and crying about how her mom's priceless antique bowl was now gone forever, because the cat had destroyed it. But don't you see? I'm the one who destroyed it—I broke the bowl! Cause if I hadn't've drank so much the night before, I wouldn't've had to pee so badly, I wouldn't've had to use my mom's bathroom, I wouldn't've seen the cat sleeping there, gone to pet him, et cetera, et cetera—the bowl would still be intact! But that's when I realized that this is the way the world works, y'know? You, you sneeze and a person dies. You leave your book on the bus, and a war breaks out! I mean if one thing leads to another, how can you do anything? How can you get up in the morning, say hi to someone, eat a meal? I move my hand this way and somewhere a kid starts crying! So of course life is monotonous! I mean we have no choice but to be as monotonous as possible! Because if we're not—if I keep drinking and peeing without thinking of anyone else—sooner or later the whole world gets destroyed!
(She leans forward.)
And I mean doesn't that scare the living shit out of you?

Information on this playwright may be found at www.smithandkraus.com. Click on the AUTHORS tab.

AMERICAN DUET

Mark Leib

Dramatic
Jessica, thirty-four

> *Jessica, a radical social worker, has been married to neo-*
> *conservative Charlie for seven years, and finally the differ-*
> *ence in their political opinions has become intolerable. The*
> *breaking point came earlier in the evening, when he gave a*
> *speech that she felt was racist and sexist and contemptuous*
> *of the plight of the poor and oppressed. So she has brought*
> *him to a dangerous tenement where she has recently worked*
> *in order to show him once and for all the America his speech*
> *ignored—and to tell him that their marriage is over.*

JESSICA: The founders, the founders, like you said in your
lecture, if we're gonna fully live up to our obligations as
Americans, the quickest way there is to turn our sights back
on the founders, okay, Old Dolly Madison and her children
live upstairs, her beloved James is in prison for seventy-five
years on two murder charges, Dolly sells blow jobs at $15 a
pop to get some food for the kids and more often to feed her
drug habit, do you know how cheap crack cocaine is, Charlie, Adam Smith wrote about it so I'm sure you're informed
on the subject. Betsy Ross lives over there, she's given her
heart to a pimp who's the love of her life, I asked her once
what she sees in him and she said, transcendence, baby,
heaven, El Dorado, the dream of George Washington as he
gazed lovingly over Mount Vernon. I can't believe that I let
you finagle me into this marriage, that you took advantage of
a damaged woman and tricked her into your callous life . . .
Oh, right, below is the room of Abigail Adams and her son
John Quincy, Abigail has four children by four lovers, she
had the children because she wanted something to belong
to her and she can't afford what she sees on television, she
has no money for food so she scavenges in garbage pails,
what welfare pays doesn't pay the rent, so she illegally takes

minimum wage jobs and swears to the government that she's unemployed, a good day for hardy Abigail is when someone brings her cheap whiskey and she can believe that she's happy living in filth and want and squalor. I already know your solution, let them fade away, let them all disappear in one final sacrifice to the holy patriarchs, to the whites and not blacks, to the men and not women, to the straights and not gays, to the English-speaking Protestants and honorary Protestants whose country we all secretly know this to be, it's frankly astonishing to me that I didn't see this part of you earlier, that I didn't know that your Paradise was the old familiar one of the alpha-males.

Information on this playwright may be found at
www.smithandkraus.com. Click on the AUTHORS tab.

American Lullaby

Cassandra Lewis

Dramatic
Faith, thirty-eight

> *The play is set in a southern plantation during a winter rain-*
> *storm. Faith (Caucasian, 38, a twice-divorced veterinarian)*
> *is caring for her father, a retired Congressman, who has*
> *just had another heart attack. A stranger, Tobias (African*
> *American, 35, college professor) has showed up at the front*
> *door, claiming to be stranded by the flood, but has just re-*
> *vealed that he was born in the Congressman's plantation.*
> *Faith recalls a time when she was a child, holding a baby*
> *that very well could have been Tobias. Her support of his*
> *claim leads to a series of disturbing revelations that change*
> *all three lives forever.*

FAITH: I remember your mother was crying. That's the last
I remember her. She was in tears and I was holding her
baby. It was a gorgeous, small little thing, with dark skin
and gray eyes. He was crying too. As I cradled him in my
arms I sang the lullaby Grandma Meri taught me and for
a moment he quieted and looked up into my eyes, like he
recognized me or maybe just the lullaby. Then Grandma
Meri—I mean Amerika Dupris—came in and took the baby
and sent me to play in my room. I don't remember anything
else, but the feeling of that day was unusual. There was a
certain sadness that day that I hadn't experienced before . .
. I learned a long time ago you got to laugh at the tragedy in
life. Otherwise, what point is there in goin' on? . . . I'm just
saying that in life—not just mine—in everybody's life—you
got all kinds of bad times. You got good times too, but way
more bad times than good. Sometimes I think the good ones
are just thrown in to torture you. To remind you of how bad
your life really is . . . I can't blame anyone but myself. But
I also think it's a lot like the state lottery. You know when
you play that you ain't gonna win and you know that even

by some chance you do win, it ain't gonna be all that much and most of it goes back to the government, anyhow. You got choices—like which numbers to pick—but ultimately the outcome is the same for everyone.

Information on this playwright may be found at www.smithandkraus.com. Click on the AUTHORS tab.

AM I BLACK ENOUGH YET?

Clinton A. Johnston

Dramatic
Shanté, twenties

> *Shanté is an African American college student. She has recently
> learned that her African American boyfriend is leaving her for
> her best friend, who is European American. Unwilling to face
> the underlying emotional reality of her situation, Shanté char-
> acterizes this betrayal solely as a racial event. This piece
> actively courts the stereotype of the "angry black woman"
> with a light comic tone until the very end (not included here)
> where Shanté's mother brings it home that this situation is, of
> course, about people falling in and losing love.*

SHANTÉ: When are we taught to hate? When are we taught to
draw lines and take sides and take things from each other?
Last Wednesday, I came to a conclusion. I concluded that I
am tired of it. I am tired of white women taking things from
me. Don't act all shocked, like you don't know what I'm
talking about, like I don't know what it's like to be the lowest
person on the totem poll? That's right. It's a fact. We come
from queens and kings who built the concept of civilization,
but you cannot get any lower in the eyes of this society than
a black woman. For instance, did you know that the majority
of people who receive assistance under the Aid to Families
with Dependant Children program or "AFDC" or, as most
people know it, "welfare" are white? Yes, that's right. Most
of welfare is going to white women . . . white women all over
the country living in urban, rural, and suburban areas. But
every time someone tries to bust on welfare, every time some
politician seeks to engender hate and disrespect, who do they
show? Some sister in a city project with four kids by three
different fathers. Why do they do that? Because they know
what we know, that nobody is lower on the unwritten social
ladder than me and my sisters. So, to return to my Wednesday epiphany, if I'm so low, why do they want to take what
little I have? They take our fashion. They take the way we

talk. They take our attitude. They even take our hairstyles. People act like Bo Derek invented corn rows. They try us on like a jacket they see in the mall and then drop us when they want to dress upscale. This is my stuff, not yours! This is my life and my culture! It is not there for you to dip into and play with whenever you get the notion. Oh, and for all of you music lovers, I hate to break it to you but Christina Aquilera is Hispanic; Mariah Carey is half black; and no matter what, my girl Ciara will always kick Britney Spears's ass just by getting up in the morning. Take that and leave my boyfriend alone!

(beat)

Last Wednesday, my boyfriend Ty comes to tell me that he and "my so-called best friend Stacy" have "developed feelings for each other." I said what about your feelings for me? And he says that's all over. He says he thinks Stacy can take him places that I can't. I told him it sounds like he wants a travel agent. That boy had the nerve to tell me I'm too angry and I don't trust people enough. I said, well I'm sorry seeing as there's obviously nothing to support not trusting your lying ass. You better go ahead and run to your little white girl who's too afraid to call you the shiftless nigger you are. But, we will leave him behind for a moment. Don't worry. He will get his. I want to focus on her. She sees me Thursday, turns around and runs away all crying and everything. It's a good thing she ran. I would have given Little Miss Ally McBeal something to cry about. What kind of low, trifling, hair-dye, piece of white trash sticks her skinny little ass in my business. He was my man! Truth be told, he wasn't much, but he was mine! Now, it's hard, it is so hard, to find a halfway decent brother to spend time with. On top of that, I've got to worry about some white chick pulling him away every time she catches a little bit of jungle fever! Dammit, I was almost done breaking him in! Now what am I going to do with him once you've used him up and tossed him aside? You're gonna' take what you want, but why do you want him? Can't you at least leave us our men?

Information on this playwright may be found at www.smithandkraus.com. Click on the AUTHORS tab.

Am I Black Enough Yet?

Clinton A. Johnston

Comic
Lola Bindeson, forties

> *Lola is the mayor of Pearl River, MI, officially the "whitest city in the U.S." ever since the eastern part of town (where all the non-white people lived) broke off to form its own burg. Seeing investment and tourism in Pearl River drop due to their lack of "ethnic flare," Lola and other town leaders have hatched a plan. They've hired African American, Antoine "Twan" Murphy ostensibly as their town web designer but actually to count his entire multi-racial background to boost town diversity numbers. This monologue is the piece's climactic moment, where Lola brings the town's racist sheriff, Curt Angstrom, into line. Lola is written for a strong north Michigan accent.*

LOLA: You stay right there, Twan! Now you listen here, Curtis Angstrom. We knew you'd have the hardest time with this, and that's why you're here right now so's we could get this whole thing straight. I'm behind this and the Town Council's behind this and the Chamber of Commerce is behind it too. Pearl River is not gonna be some backwater, whitebread town that time forgot. We're gonna have people think twice before they tell Polish jokes. We're gonna have convenience stores owned by people with funny accents. We're gonna be able to pick up a phone and order some goddamned Chinese food from across the goddamned street! Goddammit, we're gonna be diversified! And if it takes a little kick-start to make that happen, then that is what it takes! Now, you can either get on board this train or after the next elections you can be sure you will find yourself with a whole lot more time to go ice fishing. Who knows? That might be the only way you can put meat on your table. Comprende?

Information on this playwright may be found at
www.smithandkraus.com. Click on the AUTHORS tab.

ANY DAY NOW

Nat Cassidy

Comic
Jackie, early twenties.

> *At the start of this three-act play, small numbers of the recently deceased have begun reanimating and rising from their graves, and now the media and the public at large are disturbed and confused as to what this phenomenon means. Unlike the zombies of pop entertainment, however, these "returned decedents" (as they soon become known) have so far proven to be completely harmless. Just conscious-less, walking corpses. That is, until a frustrated local Connecticut politician, Beverly Colby-Parker, claims that the reanimated corpse of her father has just attacked and bitten her. She is rushed to the hospital amid a media frenzy and quickly embraces her newfound fame by holding passionate press conferences to growing crowds on the steps of the hospital, calling for martial law to destroy these so-called monsters. In this scene at the top of Act Two, while Beverly is still in the hospital, her daughter Jackie (who was just expelled from college for selling weed) visits April, Beverly's sister, in the family's kitchen where the entirety of the play takes place.*

JACKIE: Everything I know I've heard through the news, or whatever. I haven't gotten the chance to talk to her at all— I've called a bunch of times, but she's never there.
(beat)
This has all worked out pretty well for her, though, right? Rinky-dink little shit politician from nowhere, and now look at her. Like, not two weeks, and she's already, what, like a spokesperson? I'm hearing her name used as, like, a reference. I see her face on CNN, with her stupid fucking doctor, and her stupid fucking arm: "Our government must act now!" rah-rah-rah. With that smile—don't you hate that smile? I call it the shark mouth. The way it just doesn't quite reach her eyes, you know? It's so vapid and insincere. Creeps me out.

(Laughs)

She's like the Paris Hilton of the zombie apocalypse. Think about it! Professor Matos says that Paris Hilton represents the culmination of the undoing of feminism through the embrace of victimization. Fame was literally thrust into her—it wasn't until a forcible injection of the masculine that she was deemed worthy of our attention. She's celebrated for being a receptacle for semen. A gift bestowed by the patriarchy. Ipso facto, mom has become a sensation solely because of also being penetrated by a man. Granted, by his teeth, but still. Professor Matos is the greatest professor of all time. It's true! I had him for that Problems of Evil class I told you about? Critical Cultural Concepts? He, like, changed my life. And check it: "Man, so long as he lives, has no more constant and agonizing anxiety than to find someone to worship as soon as possible." It's Dostoevsky. It's from "The Grand Inquisitor." We were about to read it before I got the ol' . . .

(She cocks a thumb back and blows a raspberry).

Professor Matos just sent me an e-mail with the page number and a message saying, "Bet this is starting to ring some bells." He's so funny. But isn't it perfect? I'm thinking of getting it tattooed it on my chest, right here, so that next time Mom has a little rally with all her freaky fans, I can flash my tits at the cameras and get the message out.

Information on this playwright may be found at
www.smithandkraus.com. Click on the AUTHORS tab.

Any Day Now

Nat Cassidy

Seriocomic
Beverly, late forties to early fifties

At this point, the end of Act Two, Beverly is a full-fledged minor celebrity. She has been released from the hospital, brandishing her "bitten" arm like a badge of honor. What she has not told anyone, though, is that she faked the wound by biting a chunk out of her own arm and has been lying about the attack this whole time. However, when she returns home, she discovers that her mother somehow hid the reanimated body of her father from the authorities and has been sheltering him in the house ever since. Beverly is appalled and wounded that no one in the family believes her and so she calls another of her press conferences, whereupon she begins to reveal several family secrets in the midst of a passionate stump speech.

BEVERLY: Hi, everybody. Sorry to keep you waiting. Anyway, as you all know, I was released from the hospital today after all that extensive clinical testing. And I'm doing good. Except, on my way home, I stopped at my mother's house—the place where I was viciously attacked by one of those things. First off, I want to say that I'm saddened by the number of photographers and press waiting outside there—my mother is going through a very difficult time right now and doesn't need that stress. All inquiries about me should be made to me. I hope that's understood. Anyway, when I got there, I found that my mother was housing—hiding—the creature that did this to me
(She holds up her arm).
So, I want you all to know, I have reported the incident to 811. And I'm sure she'll do all she can to prevent his retrieval. My mother, unfortunately, is going senile. I didn't mention this in any of my recent statements, because I was trying to respect her privacy. However, I feel it's illustrative of a greater point. When she found my father, the first thing she did was . . .

(A moment of overwhelming emotion hits her. She quickly composes herself.)

I'm sorry. The first thing she did was . . . get in the shower with him. To clean him. It is absolutely tragic. Her mind is going, and it is going quickly. It seems to me that our society is showing a similar lapse in judgment. You see, my mother is suffering from the delusion that my father has come back from the dead. That, if she cleans him up, she can reenter him into society. That's not the case. My father is dead. All of our loved ones who have passed—they're still dead. There is no coming back.

Information on this playwright may be found at www.smithandkraus.com. Click on the AUTHORS tab.

Any Day Now

Nat Cassidy

Seriocomic
April, late forties to early fifties

> *After her soon-to-be ex-husband Josh's sudden suicide
> (brought about by Beverly's public airing of the family's dirty
> laundry), April's bubbly and capricious personality begins to
> slip into dazed, catatonic, almost zombie-like distraction. She
> becomes obsessed with scouring the Internet for information
> about the greater meaning of the zombie phenomenon and
> discovers that every major religion predicts the reanimation
> of the dead. Here, at the top of Act Three, only a few days
> after Josh's death, she sits in the kitchen with a Bible and
> numerous printouts from online sources, and tells Jackie and
> David (Beverly's husband) what she's figured out.*

APRIL: You wanna know what's going on? What I *think* is
   happening?
   (beat)
   All this stuff I'm reading. All these things I've been hearing
   about on the news . . . The Bible talks about the days of
   creation, right? The 7 days when the world was made? And
   all those things I mentioned, the Talmud stuff particularly,
   those are all about the Day of Judgment. Well, "day" is a
   relatively relative term. I mean, we're not talking calendar
   days, here. It's not a 24-hour span. God didn't even create
   the sun until the 4th "Day." So it's an era sort of thing. A
   period. And that's what this is. The Period of Judgment.
   I'm not trying to sound like some born again nutjub. I'm
   not gonna rush out and buy poster board and a "We Are
   Damned" stencil set. But . . .
   (almost joyfully)
   we are being judged. Can't you feel it? Judged by our
   response to this. The Lord, I don't know which Lord, is
   watching us, seeing what we're going to do. I just . . . I
   know it. Like I know Josh is going to return any day now.

You know all those zombie movies you've been watching lately? Zombies make a great metaphor. About things that don't stay buried, or about conformity or fascism. But most of all, they represent what we do to ourselves as people. How we eat each other alive, how we turn against each other indiscriminately. How even the people that we love can end up being the ones that devour us. But the "things" we're dealing with now aren't like that. They're benign. They're peaceful. And that's what convinced me. They're harmless—They're harmless. They're a reminder that we are . . . that we are good, and pure, and peaceful creatures at heart. See, I had this dream. It was beautiful, Jackie, I wish you could've seen it. God came to me. Like in "The Grand Inquisitor." And he was so beautiful and kind. And he told me that we don't have to be afraid of this. He told me that the real monsters are the hate and the rage and the inhumanity we hold in ourselves. He said, "This is your test. If there's any Armageddon, it will come from the living. From that living anger. It spreads like a disease." But the examples we are receiving are the opposite, you see? And we are being judged on how we welcome that example. I'm . . . I'm pretty sure.

Information on this playwright may be found at www.smithandkraus.com. Click on the AUTHORS tab.

BECHNYA

Saviana Stanescu

Seriocomic
Shari, early thirties, dark-haired, strong accent

Shari is in a prison in Bechnya, talking to her long absent little sister.

SHARI: The truth is . . . I didn't expect more Vickys, I always thought of just one—you, Fatma. My guy at the Embassy got me a list with Bechnyan girls adopted by Americans. 37 girls were adopted that year—can you believe that? And three of them got the name Victoria on their new birthdays . . . One in New York. One in New Jersey. One in Springville, Utah. Which one is Fatma, Vicky? *(beat)* Vicky from Utah died when she was 7. Leukemia. She couldn't be Fatma, there was no leukemia in our family. Or was it?
(She messes her hair. Helplessness.)
Rapunzel, Rapunzel! Let down your hair! . . . Rapunzel, Rapunzel . . . Let down your hair . . . Rapunzel, Rapunzel! Let down, let down, let down . . .
(beat)
It's OK, Fatma, it's OK . . . Don't get upset. Three Vickys is fine. Perfect. You're one of them. Or all of them. Or none of them. In the English language all those three statements can be true at the same time.
(She runs her fingers rhythmically through her hair. She calms down. She smiles.)
Did I tell you that an American man taught me English? And sex. But nobody should know about the sex, only about the English . . . I can die now: I had English and I had sex!
(She laughs.)
Yes, I knew the fairy tales by heart but I couldn't make any conversation. He taught me "to express my thoughts in an articulate way." Well, I wouldn't express all my thoughts, but. He was helpful. He works for the American Embassy, in Belajevo . . . He's not gonna marry me, no. He's gonna try to forget we ever talked.

(beat)

No, it wasn't love. Love doesn't exist, not even in fairy tales, didn't you notice that? It's never love, it's always about fighting for a princess' hand because it comes with half of the kingdom. It's about wealth, yes, and beauty, maybe. Sex—surely, but not love. Nobody talks about love in fairy tales, they talk about winning the princess. It's about blood. And death. And one line about happiness at the end. But who believes that. Nobody lives happily ever after.

(beat)

What's your weapon of choice, Rapunzel?—the witch asked. Grenade. No, grenades are too messy. A gun. Witch, give me a gun. A silver gun. I could use a gun right now. I would comb my hear with it. I would play Russian Roulette. Many times. Until the bullet agrees to penetrate me. Cosmic orgasm. Bliss. End.

Information on this playwright may be found at
www.smithandkraus.com. Click on the AUTHORS tab.

BLAME IT ON BECKETT

John Morogiello

Seriocomic
Tina, 65

> *Tina Fike, a famous playwright, tries to convince a young
> dramaturg, Heidi, not to abandon a theatrical career despite
> a humiliating series of professional defeats.*

TINA: Listen. Forty years ago, when I first started, ninety-nine
percent of the American public had no idea what a dramaturg was. Today that number is down to ninety-eight
percent. Depressing? For you, probably. But not when
you consider that most of the American public has no idea
what a director does, or that no one can name ten living
playwrights. It's just the nature of the beast. Theater means
nothing anymore. It's the worst field trip you ever took in
high school. It's the blow-off course you took in college
for an A. We all know this. We don't come right out and
say it to each other, but deep down we know it to be true.
People don't *choose* to work in the theater. They don't
ponder what profession will result in a lifetime of rejection,
no money, and even less recognition or advancement, and
then actively pursue it. The choice is made for them. It's a
calling, like being a priest but with a lot more sex. Come to
think of it, that's an accurate analogy. The Catholic church
is a lot like theater. Both deal with our place in society and
the universe. Both concentrate their wealth and power in a
single city—New York, Rome—while the outlying organiza-
tions are forced to scramble for donations. And both have seen
declining attendance over the last hundred years. But they
keep going. What I write is the gospel. The director is the
priest, the actors are the altar servers. The dramaturg is the
prophet. You assist the gospel writer, you help the priest
interpret the holy text, you write epistles expounding your
faith. You are misunderstood. Ignored. And sometimes?
You're martyred. Prophets lead horrible lives. Nobody

chooses to become a prophet. They choose *not* to become prophets. This is the choice you need to make.

Information on this playwright may be found at
www.smithandkraus.com. Click on the AUTHORS tab.

CALL ME WALDO

Rob Ackerman

Seriocomic
Cynthia, forties

> *Cynthia works as an attending physician at a hospital on
> Long Island. She's speaking to a nurse who has fallen in love
> with the ideas of great American philosopher Ralph Waldo
> Emerson. Cynthia tosses a verbal bucket of cold water in the
> nurse's face in an attempt to wake her up to the destructive
> nature of such thinking.*

CYNTHIA: You've been *conned.* That's what happened. You've
been seduced by aphorisms. Bumper stickers—Emerson
wrote bumper stickers before there were bumpers. He took
long walks around Walden Pond and got all amped on
endorphins and jotted down his thoughts, his deep truths,
and women loved it. Lots of women. Like Margaret Fuller.
Margaret Fuller went on those walks with Waldo, and slept
in his guest bedroom next to his study, and Margaret Fuller
was probably fucking Waldo every chance she got. Margaret
Fuller was Emerson's mistress! You don't know Emerson,
Sarah. I *know* Emerson. He was *hospitable.* He was tall and
captivating, famous and successful, with thoughtful eyes,
expressive hands, an enchanting voice, and everyone wanted
to be near him. And he wanted them all there with him, at
his table, in Concord—the barefoot bearded men and the cute
young girls like Anna Barker and Louisa May Alcott and
Caroline Sturgis—His adorable intern. He just had to have
Caroline there for inspiration, along with the cook and the
servants, and he wanted everyone to sleep over, especially
the ones to whom he was sexually attracted. It is true. But
Emerson had a family, not just a dead wife named Ellen,
but a living wife named Lidian, the mother of his children,
and Lidian wasn't happy with all the groupies in the house.
She got tired. She got testy. And, one by one, the transcen-
dentalist experiments failed. The newsletter FAILED. The

communes FAILED. The idea itself FAILED. I hate to burst your little bubble, Sarah, but Emerson was a failure. While the nation built factories and railroads, he was babbling about nature. While the scientists made great discoveries, he was waxing poetic. The transcendentalists turned into a joke, a laughing stock. Even Poe and Melville and Alcott made fun of them. I'm trying to help you, Sarah. It's unhealthy, all this heavy breathing, this wallowing in the bog of Waldo. It's a mess, that's all it is, like a male orgasm, and you can never get the stain out of the mattress. Who reads Emerson anymore anyway? They quote him, they don't read him. He's not relevant. He's not worth the *havoc* he's wreaking upon your life. You've gotta get out of Waldo World 'cause, trust me, it'll only get worse.

Information on this playwright may be found at
www.smithandkraus.com. Click on the AUTHORS tab.

CARNIVAL ROUND THE CENTRAL FIGURE

Diana Amsterdam

Seriocomic
Sheila, thirties

*Sheila is addressing, but not often looking at, her dying hus-
band—the Central Figure—in a hospital bed near her. This is
the opening speech of the play. It establishes this character's
use of small talk as an escape from the reality of her husband's
condition; she needs to keep the small talk flowing.*

SHEILA: You were a hundred percent right. They do clean
up much better. I barely have to run a mop over them.
Sometimes I add a little Step Saver. But I really don't have
to. Mother couldn't believe it. I told her it was your idea. I
gave you full credit! And it was so smart not to get white!
When I think now that we lived all those years with white
kitchen tiles! Were we crazy? Of course, you said and said
and said. Of course I wouldn't listen. What is that surface?
What's it called? Well, it's not all nubbly. Why they want to
make kitchen tiles all nubbly is something I will never know.
I know. Because they think that way the dirt will be camou-
flaged. Huh! What they fail to understand is that there are
still certain people who notice that every day, the number of
nubblies strangely increases! Yes! Till there are thousands of
nubblies! Only it's not nubblies! It's dirt! Yes! Dirt! Only by
then the dirt is so ingrained you can't get it out! Remember
all the toothbrushes we went through? Lucky thing Mother's
Mah Jong crowd saved their toothbrushes, did you ever write
Mrs. Roseverweiss that thank-you note? It doesn't matter.
She moved to Florida. The important thing is that when you
come home this time, you will never, never have to scrub the
kitchen floor with a toothbrush ever again! Isn't that wonderful? Just barely moisten the mop and voila!

*Information on this playwright may be found at
www.smithandkraus.com. Click on the AUTHORS tab.*

Carnival Round The Central Figure

Diana Amsterdam

Dramatic
MaryAnn, thirties to sixties

*Maryann can be any age from 30 to 60. She is a commanding
woman with a strong sense of purpose, who believes in posi-
tive thinking—that we create our own destinies and therefore
can defeat even death. This monologue takes place at one of
her many lectures, when she speaks to families of patients
and professional colleagues at Memorial Grace Hospital,
where she is a psychologist.*

MARYANNE: I am not particularly worried about global warming. I am a firm believer that every woman has the right to
an abortion. I am a vegetarian. I am a libertarian. I am a
lazy son of a bitch. I am an accountant. I am an artist. I am
a Christian. I am a Muslim. I am a dreamer. I am a realist. I
am a husband. I am a child. I am. These two words and your
faith in them are the great fortress that stands between you
and Death. We sit in our chairs. Cloaked and wrapped and
defined in our personal I am's. We cannot begin to imagine
the agony of the dying person. And this is how it should
be. We are meant to live in the belly of a profound compla-
cency. But the dying person? He or she is stripped of every
defense. In the course of the diagnosis, the hospitalization,
the drugs, the pity and the pain, the dying person suffers
the loss of each and every I am till only one remains. I am
alive. And then, that too dissolves, like a teardrop in the
ocean. Except for the survivor! The survivor either from
stupidity or the most profound courage refuses to give up
his last remaining I am. I am alive!

*Information on this playwright may be found at
www.smithandkraus.com. Click on the AUTHORS tab.*

CLOSE UP SPACE

Molly Smith Metzler

Dramatic
Vanessa, thirties-forties

> *Vanessa Finn Adams, a best-selling novelist, is confronting*
> *her editor, Paul, who has come into his office and found that*
> *it's been completely cleaned out—by his mentally unstable*
> *daughter Harper, who has taken the manuscript of Vanessa's*
> *latest novel (the only copy). She is already angry because*
> *Paul has gutted her novel. Now Vanessa is really pissed that*
> *he seems to have lost it.*

VANESSA: You left my manuscript unattended—unlocked—in
this piece of shit office is what you did. Do you have any
idea how hard my life has been? Do you have any idea how
hard it has been for me to get here? The discipline and the
loneliness I have endured in order to keep myself in a state
of open vessel-hood for the faeries and magic of creativ-
ity? I have suffered the slings and arrows of outrageous
misfortune in my life and you have so little respect for my
work that you would leave it unattended in a generic office
building in Midtown?! Midtown?! Harper . . . is a sweet-
heart. She's the angel who returned it to me. She showed up
at my apartment and woke me up, and I grew to like her so
much that I opened my last bottle of 85 Corton-Charlemagne
Vielles Vignes Grand Cru that I had been saving for Garth's
wedding and we drank it. We talked for over an hour, your
daughter and I. [in English] And French. And Greek qua-
trains. There were fresh tears in her eyes when she showed
up. And in the morning mist, with her little hat, it was all
very Doctor Zhivago, and she looked up at me and she said,
"Hello, Vanessa Finn Adams, I'm Harper Hayes, Gloria
Hayes' daughter. My Mom was a big admirer of your work
and considered you an unrivalled peer. I can see from your
handwritten notes that you're working on this novel so I
am returning it to you because . . . ."

(voice breaking, overwhelmed with emotion)
. . . Sorry. Just a moment . . .
(resuming)
"I am returning it to you because I think you have written the feminine anthem of your generation. But please keep it away from my Dad because he's definitely over-editing you." I'll tell you what's ridiculous, Paul. It's ridiculous that your daughter understands what you don't: that my scribbles deserve a 42 block walk in the middle of the night. That my scribbles are religious, and dangerous, and necessary. Your daughter understands what a magnificent gesture of trust it is to show someone your work, and ask them to hold it, and hear it, and respond to it. You should be ashamed of yourself, the way you've treated her. The poor thing doesn't have a Mom, Paul, and she's sending you poems, desperately trying to get your attention. Don't you know how hard that is to do!?

COMPLETENESS

Itamar Moses

Dramatic
Molly, twenties

Molly, a graduate student in molecular biology, is conflicted about her feelings for Eliot, a graduate student in computer science and her supposed boyfriend.

MOLLY: This is what it's like. It's like you walk off down the road. And you think you're making all this progress. And then you stop, and look down, and you're like, oh: he is the road. And so then the question becomes: what am I supposed to do? Like, does that mean I shouldn't try again, or that I definitely should, like, right away? Like, is waiting the answer, or is it the problem because the answer is not waiting? And if I don't know then how am I supposed to tell somebody else I want to be with him and mean it? And, if I do like someone, and if that makes me forget my sadness for a while, then does that mean that that guy make me happy? Or does that just mean that, once that fades, once he's not useful anymore, for like masking or replacing all my pain, then nothing will be left, except this guy who through no fault of his own will just be, like, repellent to me now, because he's just this other thing, with all of its own crap to deal with, just this extra burden on what I was carrying already? Or, if is this actually just unfixable now, if these feelings are just a part of me? Then is the right person someone who can just accept and live with them? And even if I find someone who can, what if I can't? Like, what if that's not how I want to live? Like. What if there's a place in you that's only really touched when you get hurt. And nothing else can touch you in that place. But certain things pretend they can, and so your choices are to believe until you can't anymore, and really hurt someone, and I've really hurt some people, or to keep believing, to make yourself believe, and then get hurt yourself, again, in that same place? Or does the fact that that's what all this taught me mean that I've been doing absolutely all of it in some way wrong, that there's some other, better, way to do it, and that, every time, there is at least the chance I'll finally figure out what other way that is? *(beat)* You know?

Information on this playwright may be found at
www.smithandkraus.com. Click on the AUTHORS tab.

CUT

Crystal Skillman

Dramatic
Rene, thirty-one

In Cut three reality TV show writers (Danno, Colette and Rene) are forced to re-cut the season finale to their Housewives rip-off "The Ladies of Malibu" in three hours which forces them to confront the real truth of how their destructive actions over the past six weeks have affected each other. Here, Rene is forced to face the truth of her own life falling apart as she does a "pick up interview" with Jessica, one of the housewives.

RENE: I'm like ok: we're going to cut to this interview right after you get the divorce call from your husband, so you shouldn't be smiling ok? And I swear to god. That grin, it doesn't come off and she's like what? And I'm like: THIS IS LIKE EMOTIONAL SHIT OK? It's time to let it hang out. And she's like: "I'm getting a lot of money. The settlement."
For a second I see my daughter: I see her bank account. Zero. Maybe Jessica you can talk more? Maybe—Maybe you can share what it's like when the man you love tells you are nothing like who he fell in love with? How all the affairs were your fault because you're hard and uncaring, even though you paid his fucking air fare to London with your shit job. About how in the middle of the night you cross the earth and right here—last chance—but all the time you feel Danno . . . holding you. Jessica she just: "You have to be your best self, pick yourself up, be nice to yourself in times of tragedy." There are no tears, no—And I hate myself—I hate myself when my first thought is we'll have to cut in Colette's earlier footage of Jessica crying after losing her dog in her backyard for a half hour.
Because the audience will need that. They want that.
(breaking)
I respect myself for knowing I can do that.

ELECTRA

Don Nigro

Seriocomic
Lexie Ryan, twenty-eight

> *Lexie is smart and attractive, with a quick mind and a dark
> sense of humor. She is the middle child of Carolyn and the
> late Michael Ryan, a banker. Her older sister Jenna is in the
> madhouse for killing their father in the bathtub with a pair
> of scissors while she was giving him a haircut, but Lexie is
> convinced that in fact their mother Carolyn killed him for
> the insurance money, then blamed it on her already mentally
> troubled daughter. Their younger brother Thomas, long be-
> lieved to be dead, is just back from the First World War, and is
> deeply traumatized by his experiences there. Lexie has taken
> him to the cemetery to visit their father's grave. She is trying
> to work up the courage to reveal to him the truth about her
> father's death, and to convince him to help her murder their
> mother and her lover Nick.*

LEXIE: There it is. That little mound of earth, under the wild
cherry tree. They still haven't put the stone up. The man
who does the tombstones caught his wife in bed with a Bible
salesman and tried to carve a derogatory inscription on
her backside and in the ruckus they knocked over a candle
and set the house on fire, and the Bible salesman burned to
death hiding in the fruit cellar, so the tombstone carver's
in jail for manslaughter, and our father's grave is still just
marked by a little pile of dirt. That's the sort of thing that
happens around here. Dark low comedy. Mother ordered a
megalith the size of Stonehenge to impress the neighbors,
but almost nobody speaks to us now. People stare at us on
the street and mutter at each other like extras in a bad Greek
chorus. Mother used to enjoy so much wringing her hands
and wailing over and over, my son is dead, my son is dead.
She likes to hear the sound of her own voice so it drowns
out any attempt to think on her part or anybody else's. But
here you are, and it's Papa who's dead. I still can't believe

you're here. But everything seems like a dream now. Even the birds are strange since he died. I don't like the way they look at me. There's something wrong with the crows. I wake up in the morning and everything seems just slightly out of place. I look at the trees and think, did somebody move them over night? Do the trees walk around all night and then never quite get back in exactly the right places? Everything here is *Through The Looking-Glass.* I wonder where Loopy Rye is today. You know things are bad when the village idiot is ashamed to be seen with you. It's going to rain again. It always rains now. God, I hate monologues. Please say something so I can shut the hell up.

Electra

Don Nigro

Seriocomic
Carolyn Ryan, forty-seven

> *Carolyn is the widow of Michael Ryan, a successful small town banker, whom she has inadvertently killed while trying to prevent him from committing suicide in his bath with a pair of scissors. She has successfully lied to the sheriff, convincing him that her mentally disturbed daughter Jenna did it, knowing that Jenna would be put back in the madhouse and Carolyn would get the insurance money. But the guilt is beginning to prey upon Carolyn's mind, and she is starting to hear strange noises, flapping and buzzing sounds. She is intelligent and has a dark sense of humor but is very highly strung, the pressure is getting to her, and here she is talking to herself on the front porch swing one night, trying to maintain control of her mind. Another secret she is keeping is that she is actually the love child of the village idiot, Loopy Rye. Also on her mind here are her other daughter Lexie, whom she knows suspects the truth and fears will try and kill her, her son Thomas, just back from the First World War and deeply traumatized, her drunken lover Nick, who is Jenna's husband, the notoriously crooked bank president Harry MacBeth, who she believes is out to get her, and the imaginary crocodile Jenna always feared was hiding under her bed. This is a strong and stubborn woman, under tremendous strain and racked with guilt, trying hard to stay sane and gradually losing the battle.*

CAROLYN: Which is not to say I'm not perfectly fine, because I am fine, for a woman whose insane daughter has stuck her husband in the neck with a pair of scissors in the bath tub. I'm a strong, powerful woman who's taken charge of her life. And I'm not ashamed to say that—What the hell are all those damned flapping noises? What is it? Who are you? Bats? Are you bats? What's flapping? Who's whispering?

What is all this damned whispering about? Will you children be quiet and go to sleep? There is no damned crocodile under the bed. I just need to get some rest. Loopy? I know you're out there listening. Damned village idiot. And that crooked son of a bitch Harry MacBeth is trying to push Nick out of the bank. Nobody will talk to us. People point and whisper on the street. The house is falling apart. I'm going to end up jabbering in the graveyard with Loopy if I don't watch out. You're not my father. The village idiot is not my father. Last night I dreamed I gave birth to a snake. I wrapped it in Tommy's baby blanket and let it suck at my breasts, and it drew clotted blood with the milk. I have suckled monsters. Jenna was sweet but always teetering at the edge of some precipice or other. Lexie was more self reliant but she asked too many damned questions. Intelligence in children is always a sign of bad things to come. Thomas was a train wreck. Such nightmares. Giant insects eating him. Drowning in vats of blood. I'd ask myself, who are these bizarre creatures who've crawled out of my body? And is there any way I can put them back and exchange them for something else? Some sort of washing machine? But redemption comes from within. In other words, there is none. I feared as much.

(She notices someone standing in the shadows.)

Who is that? Why is there always somebody standing over there in the dark? We need to get a god damned street light put in down here.

ELECTRA

Don Nigro

Seriocomic
Carolyn Ryan, forty-seven

Carolyn Ryan is a strong and intelligent but troubled woman who has accidentally murdered her husband Michael in the bathtub with a pair of scissors when he was trying to commit suicide, then blamed her allegedly mad daughter Jenna for killing him so Carolyn could collect the insurance money. Carolyn knows that her other daughter, Lexie, has been trying to convince her youngest child, Thomas to kill her, to avenge her father's murder. Thomas is just back from World War I, is in despair, very unstable, and in Carolyn's mind perhaps quite capable of violence against her. This night on the porch, Thomas has just asked her, point blank, if she murdered his father. This is Carolyn's reply. She is struggling here to remain calm and reassure him, but she is so distraught that what comes out is only making things worse.

CAROLYN: How can you ask me a question like that? I loved your father very deeply. I love him even more now that he's dead. What I mean is, I appreciate him more, now that he isn't here. Not that I want him not to be here. I mean, I don't want him here if he's dead. That wouldn't be very pleasant. But fortunately, he is dead. What I mean is, if he wasn't dead, I'd want him here, and I'm sure I'd appreciate him a lot more than I did when he was alive, which was a lot, although he did get on my nerves sometimes, especially when I'd ask him a question and he'd just stare at the wallpaper, but then, so did my children, and I still love all of you. Some more than others. Maybe you most of all, in fact. Not that I don't love your sisters. I don't like them, but I do love them. If I didn't love them, I'd have killed them a long time ago, because I'm pretty sure they both want to kill me. I'm speaking metaphorically here. I know your sisters wouldn't really kill me. Well, Jenna can't kill me. She's in the looney bin. Lexie did try to push me off the roof, but I think she was just horsing around. It's hard to tell with her. She seems more sane, but I think it's all an act. She might actually be the craziest of the bunch. Not that I think you're crazy. A little strange, maybe. But everybody around here is strange. Lately even I've been a little strange. I know that's hard to believe, but I've been hearing things. I can't tell you what a relief it is that you're hearing things, too. The family that has hallucinations together can make that sort of thing a bonding experience. I know you and I haven't done much bonding. The last time I felt you really wanted to be close to me was when you were nursing. And you used to bite me. My nipples are still sore. But you probably don't want to talk about my nipples. I don't even want to talk about my nipples. Your father used to talk about my nipples. But nursing three children really knocked the hell out of my breasts. I wanted to get a wet nurse but I was afraid your father would want to suck on her too. I never did trust him. You're the only person around here I've ever been able to trust, and maybe that's just because half the time we hardly noticed you. You hardly ever said a word. We actually thought you were simple minded until your father realized you were reading Sophocles in the original. You were fourteen years old and we weren't even sure you spoke English. You have an amazing gift for languages, for somebody who could go for months without talking to anybody but the cat. I know it might have seemed like I was neglecting you when you were growing up, but that was because your sisters were driving me berserk.

First Base Coach

Jerrod Bogard

Dramatic
Amy, eleven

*Amy is a precocious, TV-educated latch-key kid. 9 year-old
Ben has heard when a guy goes out with a girl he's supposed
to "go the bases." Not knowing what that means, he's at the
mercy of the more experienced 11 year-old Amy when the
two meet on the neighborhood baseball diamond. On first
base Amy explains that they're supposed to switch jackets. At
second base, she says, is where they tell a secret. Here Amy
tells Ben a secret about her first experience with death.*

AMY: *(defensively)*I didn't kill it. It died on it's own. Suffocated.
I don't know. Thirty six days. I thought it would die in like
a day. After four days though it was just really mad. And I
know why. I knew why. I put it under glass. It couldn't fly.
It couldn't pollinate flowers or make honey or do any bee
stuff bees are meant to do. I impeded its beeness. Do you
know what impeded means? It started to calm down after
a week, and then one day it didn't move so I thought—you
know. So I scooted the glass toward the edge of the table,
to—and it moved. Nope, wasn't dead yet. I checked on it
everyday. I'd think it was dead and then it would move.
And then I would think it was dead and start to move the
jar and then it would move again. It was so mad and so sad
and so angry and so. And it wouldn't just- just-just-just die.
And I—so I came home every day and I sit at my desk . .
. and I would talk to it. I said, "Die. Please die. Please die
little bee." Like that. Why'd it have to come in my room
in the first place? Tell me that. You can't. Nobody can. On
the 36th it was twitching one leg real slow, and when it
stopped? I cried harder than I ever cried that day. I knew
the whole time I could've let it go so easy, and I buried it
in my dad's garden where he used to grow peppers. Why
did I do that?

First Day of School

Billy Aronson

Seriocomic
Kim, thirty to forty

Kim is a married parent who is treasurer of the elementary school PTA. David, another married parent, has invited her to have sex with him. In this monologue, Kim bursts into David's house and informs him that she has decided to accept his offer. Since Kim is a moral, sensitive, thoughtful individual, she is unable to discuss explicitly the act in which she is anxious to engage. So she speaks in a kind of improvised code.

KIM: I'm sorry David but I find it insanely ridiculous that kids in our day had choir and orchestra and band and jazz ensemble but our kids have a chorus led by a science teacher and that's it, so they'll never know that thrill of discovering music with their peers, you remember that total rush, right?, you're squishing your fingers into the holes and blowing til you're dizzy and there's spit flying everywhere and you're thinking this is stupid I can't believe they're making me do this and then suddenly my god you can't believe such glorious music is really coming from you and these friends you'll have forever. So the thing is I've found a matching grant that can get us guitars, violins, a few horns, a drum set, and someone to teach the kids and enter them in festivals but we don't stand a chance, it's slipping away, we're dead in the water unless we can get major community support and now. I can't do it on my own, David. I have tried and I have tried. I need you to sit with me and brainstorm ideas, and please hear me out because it's scary, I know. You want a guarantee that it'll happen and you won't just be sitting there in the dark but I'm telling you David it's a mystery, it has to be, okay? I can't know just how it'll go, we have to sit there and sweat it out, and to be honest with you I can't imagine it, but I have to believe there's a way to make that inconceivable leap, those things happen in life, right? You can't see your way to the next step but then you're suddenly there?, but it's impossible to reason your way across that gulf David, at some point you have to accept that it's out of your hands and just trust that if we're good people and what we're doing is deeply inspired and we just let go with what we feel and go with our impulses we have nothing to be afraid of so even though it seems like this impossible ocean we can't turn our backs David we really have to jump in and go for it because the stakes are so high.

*Information on this playwright may be found at
www.smithandkraus.com. Click on the AUTHORS tab.*

First Day of School

Billy Aronson

Seriocomic
Kim, thirty to forty

Kim is a married parent. After dropping off her children for the first day of school, she runs into David, another married parent. In the middle of a conversation about their children's schools and their spouse's careers, David asks Kim if she would like to have sex with him. In this monologue, she attempts to answer his question.

KIM: Do I want to have sex with you? Oh David. How can you ask me that? I have a husband and three children. And you have a wife and kids. What are you thinking? You seriously would just run off and do that, just like that? My god, maybe I'm naïve but I like to think that people are really with who they say they're with. I made a commitment, I'm sorry, and you made a commitment too David. When you say you're going to be with someone you should stick with them and make it work out. Yes I ran around when I was young, and that was a good time sometimes, I certainly had my good times like anybody else but you made a promise to stay with someone and you need to honor that. And sure, there are problems, there are always going to be problems. So you get counseling. You don't just chuck it for whatever's fun. And I don't even mean fun because how can it be fun sneaking around like that, ducking off somewhere. How can you even conceive of doing that, David? Where would you even go? David. "We could go to my house." Do you hear how filthy that sounds? We'd just run off to your house. In the middle of the day. An empty house in the middle of the day, lounging around naked. How awful does that sound David, how disgusting. I've got a list of school supplies to buy for the twins. I was going to try to catch up with the vice principal about music in the schools and the pumpkin drive, and I'm sorry if that sounds stupid to you David but

I'd rather be getting something accomplished than sneaking off to your house in the middle of the day, like the neighbors wouldn't notice, and talk, they would talk, or would you have me show up later? Is that what you're thinking? You'd go in and then I'd walk in separately a little later? And if anyone noticed you'd have what?, some kind of story to tell them? Is that it? You'd say we were talking about the music program, how some city fundraising program that you knew from your work could be a model for the drive I'm planning this coming October? Fine, so you'd pile one lie on top of another as you snuck around, risking causing enormous pain for these wonderful people you love and promised to honor all your life and for what David. What. Three minutes of pleasure? Ten minutes? Half an hour?

Information on this playwright may be found at
www.smithandkraus.com. Click on the AUTHORS tab.

First Day of School

Billy Aronson

Seriocomic
Alice, thirty to forty

> *Alice is a married parent. After dropping off her children
> for the first day of school, she runs into David, another mar-
> ried parent. When David asks if she would like to have sex
> with him, Alice reveals that she has been living in a world
> of imaginary romantic relationships. In this monologue, she
> considers having a relationship that isn't imaginary.*

ALICE: That's the thing. Do I throw in the towel? I'm so sick
of the games. But then you came along, right? You're really
direct which makes it easy to let things out. It's so flatter-
ing, somebody who really goes out on a limb and makes
the commitment, it's a great big pat on the back is what
it is. So even though I'm feeling all these different things
now and I'm not sure exactly where they'll land I have to
tell you that someone accepting me for who I am goes a
long way because I feel like with you it doesn't matter, you
know? That I have a hangnail on my thumb. A little bit of
hardened skin. So what. And a little scar from a sty that
was removed two years ago under my eye. Who cares. Or
that there's a crevice between two of my teeth that catches
seeds or leafs or the casing from a bean, it doesn't matter,
or that my back sweats, blotches of sweat drip down my
back, big deal, I sweat, so what, or that when I'm talking to
people I get this sense that something's hanging from my
nose so I start touching my nose over and over and then the
other person starts touching their nose and soon we're both
touching our noses and no one's enjoying what anyone is
saying so my back starts to sweat all the way down to the
back of my thighs, I have very sweaty thighs and ankles and
feet, so what, it doesn't matter that my legs sweat and my
feet sweat or that I touch my nose a lot or that when other
people are laughing I'm not laughing, they're looking at me

to laugh and I want to be laughing but I'm not laughing I'm never laughing, I'm standing there picking my thumbs and licking my teeth and sucking on my saliva and my mucous and I'm sweating, my entire body is gushing until I stink up the room and that's fine.

Information on this playwright may be found at www.smithandkraus.com. Click on the AUTHORS tab.

FLESH AND THE DESERT

Carson Kreitzer

Seriocomic
Josie, thirties to forties.

Josie is a Las Vegas Showgirl. Here, she is in her dressing room, wearing her backstage kimono, talking to a reporter doing a story on Las Vegas.

JOSIE: Soon there will be no glamour left.
One night I'm standing up there, in the dark. In my five thousand dollar Bob Mackie gown. It's topless, but it's still a gown. This gorgeous draped blue velvet, with rhinestones on it like stars.
the lights hit me and I hear this guy out in the audience
this guy comin through from bumfuck Idaho or godknows where clear as day he says
She looks just like Venus.
Now, you don't get that dancin' on a pole.
Men don't think you look like the ancient greek goddess of Love.
(listens)
Really? It's Roman? Who's the Greek—
never mind.
Anyway, you don't look like the goddess of anything, hangin' off a pole.
You look like, excuse me, but you look like you need the money.
Now don't get me wrong. We all need the money. That's why we're here.
But standing up under those lights
in a blue velvet gown with stars on it send little beams of light shooting around the gallery when you walk?
You don't feel
like you need the money not when you're up there.

You feel like maybe maybe
You're a Goddess
if their feet hurt, too.

Flesh and the Desert

Carson Kreitzer

Seriocomic
Slot Machine, ageless

> *Speaker is a slot machine at a casino in Las Vegas. Although*
> *this was played in the original production by a woman, it*
> *could just as easily be played by a man. The Slot Machine*
> *is talking to the audience as if we were someone feeding it*
> *coins.*

SLOT MACHINE: I know you're gonna get lucky this time
　　I can feel it
　　come on, this is it. This is gonna be your lucky pull.
　　Damn, well next time
　　cause you are definitely gonna win today
　　I can feel it, today
　　You are a winner
　　Pull my arm
　　Wanna drink?
　　Lemme get you a drink.
　　No, just tip the girl. I got the drink taken care of. You're
　　welcome. Anytime . . . .
　　Just give me a pull
　　and I know you're gonna get lucky
　　maybe next go-round
　　You and me, we're really connecting, here
　　you know what I mean?
　　You and me, we're a lot alike
　　One out of many, we found each other here
　　staring face to face
　　I'm yours. Your machine.
　　Your private dialogue with God.
　　Heaven and Hell. Saved or Damned.
　　Lucky or Unlucky.
　　I'm the only one who can tell you

and baby let me tell you
you are gonna be lucky, I can feel it
just one more pull's gonna set me
over the edge
spilling down coins into your waiting, grateful lap
all the coins you put in me
and all the poor suckers before you
a shower of money
coins warmed in my belly flowing out over your hands
maybe this time
maybe this time

maybe this time
hey . . . .
don't look at me that way
where you going?
Let me get you another drink
Look, I . . . .
I wasn't lying I'd never lie to you I
No I really thought . . .
I mean, you look like a lucky guy to me.
Okay, you got me that's what I tell them all
of course that's what I tell them all but with you
I really thought it
might be
true
Believe me, baby there's nothing a machine likes better
than paying out
and tonight I feel so fat and full
some lucky bastard's gonna come along
give me that pull
But you gotta go back to your room.
I understand. Really I do.
But before you go
how about just one more
gimme just one more,
(suddenly harsh, jarring:)
come on, it's only a quarter.
Yeah.
Well, I got payments to make, too.

Who do you think's paying for that Sphinx going up down the street

(She flips a coin from her hand into the air. Catches it in her mouth.)

I'll see you tomorrow, right?

GOOD PEOPLE

David Lindsay-Abaire

Dramatic
Margaret, forties

Margaret's life has been nothing but bad luck. She has recently been let go from her latest minimum wage job due to chronic tardiness caused by her difficulty in finding someone reliable to watch her severely retarded daughter. She has come to what she thought was a party at the home of an old boyfriend from high school, whose life has been an unmitigated success, in hopes that she might meet somebody who can give her a job. He has asked her why her life has been one disaster after another.

MARGARET: I didn't choose to be late. Shit happened, that made me late! Sometimes it was Joyce. Sometimes it was the T. One time I got my car taken. Why'd I lose the car? Because I missed a payment. Why'd I miss a payment? Because I had to pay for a dentist instead. Why'd I have to pay the dentist? Because I didn't have insurance, and I cracked a tooth and ignored it for six months, until an abscess formed. Why'd I crack a tooth? Because one night I thought I'd save a little money, and skip dinner! But I got hungry and decided to snack on a piece of candy brittle. And that's all it took—a piece of fucking candy brittle, and I was out of a job again. And that's how it always is. And if it's not the candy brittle then it's Joyce's medication, or my phone getting cut off, or Russell Gillis breaking in and stealing my goddamn microwave! And you wanna tell me about choices? While you sit up here practically breaking your arm patting yourself on the back for all you accomplished. Lucky you. You made some wise choices. But you're wrong if you think everyone has 'em. In fact, the only real choice I ever did make was dumping you. And yeah, I've thought about it a million times since. "What woulda happened if I hadn't dumped Mikey Dillon?" Maybe I wouldn't have ended up with Gobie, or maybe I woulda finished school, or maybe this coulda been my house. Maybe it coulda been. All of this. Maybe it coulda been mine.

Information on this playwright may be found at www.smithandkraus.com. Click on the AUTHORS tab.

Hologram

Don Nigro

Dramatic
Laura, twenty-six

> *Laura, 26, has just started graduate school and seems to be*
> *doing well, but in fact she is a troubled girl, abandoned by her*
> *parents, raised by her stepfather, Stephen, upon whom she's*
> *projected many contradictory but powerful feelings, including*
> *gratitude and love, but also anger at her parents and at him*
> *for not loving her enough, and also a deep undercurrent of*
> *suppressed erotic attachment, a feeling which Stephen shares*
> *but has been trying to fight. Here she has called him late at*
> *night and is ostensibly giving him ideas for the novel he's*
> *been writing, but in fact she's confronting him directly for*
> *the first time with the essence of their own situation. In the*
> *play, although it's presumably a phone call, no telephone is*
> *present or mimed. She is in a circle of light speaking to us*
> *as if directly to him.*

LAURA: Suppose the daughter is in love with her stepfather?
Suppose she's been waiting to grow up so she can take her
mother's place? But it isn't just her. There's a kind of conspiracy between them. Between her and the stepfather. An
unspoken conspiracy. They both know. They've known for
years. But they never talk about it. But it's always there between them. It's perfect. See, that's what drives the mother
out of her mind. That's why she goes away. She knows they
want to get rid of her. That it's not really about her at all.
It's about them. And so she gives them what they want.
It's an act of love, really. Well, a demented act of love by
a self-destructive crazy person, but then, what isn't? But
wait. This is the good part. That's what they've both been
secretly hoping, right? The daughter and the stepfather, that
the mother will go away. So she goes away and gives them
what they want, because she can't take it any more and
she's losing her mind or whatever, and the thing is, when

she actually does go away, it totally freaks them out. To get what they wanted is terrifying. And also, they're both really hurt. That she would leave them. Because her being there is what's allowed them to have this mutual fantasy that they never talk about, the fantasy that when the girl grows up she's going to marry the stepfather. It was really exciting, as long as they didn't talk about it. But now that the mother is gone and it's just them all alone in that house the both of them are terrified out of their minds. Except the stepfather is even more terrified than the daughter. What do you think?

Home of the Great Pecan

Stephen Bittrich

Comic
Priscilla, seventeen to eighteen

1983. On a Sunday afternoon in the idyllic town of Seguin, Texas, beauty queen frontrunner and high school senior Priscilla Rottweiller practices her acceptance speech in the mirror for the crowning of the city's favorite daughter, the Pecan Queen. Little does she know that soon her whole world will be thrown into horrible disarray when someone (or something) steals the symbol of the 102nd Annual Pecan Festival from the town square, the 500 pound statue of the Great Pecan.

PRISCILLA: *(presenting a delicate, thoughtful address)* Thank you. Thank you, one and all. I'd like to thank the members of the selection committee for this great honor. I am sure it could not have been an easy decision considering all of the intelligent, beautiful contenders for the crown—
(as she nods to each of the losers)
—Tawnya Blackhorn, DeAndra Loogan, Cynthia Morales. Wonderful, wonderful competitors all. I pledge that I will wear the crown of Pecan Queen with pride and distinction for the year to come. No thank you speech would be complete without thanking my dear, dear family—my baby brother, Deke, my father, head engineer of Structural Metals, Inc.—
(waving to Daddy)
Hi, Daddy. And lastly, but certainly not leastly, my mother, who, by example, has taught me the true meaning of womanhood—
(acknowledging a knock at the bathroom door, her angelic demeanor turns Satanic)
WHAAAAAAAT! Oh for the love of God, Mother, just start dinner without me! I'm in the middle of my speech! I'll be down in a minute! *Comprende inglese?*

(She lets loose a huge, painful sigh, as she tries to recompose that sweet, dutiful demeanor and remember where she left off in the speech.)

Hi, Daddy. Hi, Daddy. Hi, Daddy. And lastly, but certainly not leastly, my mother, who by example has taught me the true meaning of womanhood. *Je t'aime, ma mere.* I think it was that wise philosopher, Camus, who said, "This is the dog's dick."

(beat)

Oh, my. Did I just say, "dick?" Mercy me. I have just said "dick" and turned you all into horny toads. Dick, dick, dick. Dog's dick.

(like she is doing a newsflash)

"Pecan Queen shocks the world—says 'dick' in front of an adoring crowd of onlookers." Now that I'm Pecan Queen, there are going to be a few changes around here. First of all, DeAndra Loogan, you will carry my train for the entire year—always following a respectful twenty-eight steps behind. I have a veeery long train. Where was I? Ah, yes, of course. This will be the year when the Pecan Queen makes a difference. This will be the year when the Pecan Queen takes some action—solves World Hunger. World Peace. And combats gaucherie in all its forms. This I promise.

Information on this playwright may be found at www.smithandkraus.com. Click on the AUTHORS tab.

Hurt Village

Katori Hall

Comic
Toyia, late twenties to early thirties, African-American

Toyia is the nosy neighborhood gossip. She's having her hair done by Crank, who is 3 years clean off of crack, who hustles the government and does everybody's hair in the neighborhood. Toyia works as an exotic dancer at the local "shake junt," She's Cornbread's "babymama," considers herself a feminist.

TOYIA: TILAPIA! I know you ain't sittin on my brand new muthafuckin' Camero. I can't tell! Well, pop yo' ass right back off it then. These project kids don't know who they messin' wit. Can't wait to move out this muthafucka.
(She begins to dance and snap her fingers to the beat. Something by the R & B Pied Piper. R Kelly.)
Oooooo! I hate this song!
(She makes her booty clap on the beat.)
Trapped in the closet 44 was good though. But I got that shit free from the Bootleg man, don't play. You won't catch me buyin not a na'an 'nother R Kelly CD. I ain't got time to puttin' no scrilla in no pedophile's pockets. I'm a muthafuckin' feminist! Is that niggah ever gone go on trial? That bitch just don't wanna give up her allowance, hell, can't say I would either, but that niggah need to be put on punishment, or somethin'. She can't let him get away with that shit. She need to put him on "pussy punishment." Tru that! Shit, "pussy punishment" the next birth control. Cornbread ain't bout to burn my shake junt body out. Awww, hell to the the naw, naw, naw. But the folks up at the hospital really know about pussy punishment. Folks up there had the nerve to try to tie my tubes after I had LaQwana. Nurse come over to the bed before they give me my epidural talkin' bout, "The doctor recommends that a woman with your history try a surgical approach to birth control." She might as well said

"Nigger-bitch, we don't want y'all to be havin no mo' of yo' nigger children so we shuttin' down the reproductive power of yo' pussy!" I said, "Bitch, if you don't get them muthafuckin' papers out my muthafuckin' face I'ma stick a gun up in yo' muthafuckin' chest, and you won't be needin' no doctor after I'm finish witchu. You gone need a coroner." Hell, I raised the terror alert to red up in that bitch! But she right though. I ain't got time for na'an one mo' child. And that way Cornbread on "pussy punishment." Put some red up in my head.

Hurt Village

Katori Hall

Seriocomic
Cookie, thirteen, African-American

Cookie is precocious and gifted, a wannabe rapper who just wants to get out of the poor community where she lives. This monologue begins the play, and is direct address to the audience.

COOKIE: This be the war/ungh/this be the war/ ungh
> This be the war/ungh/this be the war/ ungh, ungh This be the war/ungh/this be the war/ ungh Ungh/
> You can't see the stars no more/
> Just the bling from the dreams of souls searching for the same thing/ For a lift of light from cavin' ceilings/
> This my ode to project people strugglin'/
> Mamas and fathers hold yo' daughters/
> I'm precocious/most here know this and they know I spit the illest shit/ I spin ghetto tales that'll make you weep/
> My lyrical lullabyes'll knock yo ass to sleep/
> Cause I be the street storyteller/
> Runnin' crackers through my hellah/
> Ringin the bells and yellin through the wire like Mariah/ Having CNN on fire/
> Bye bye to crumblin walls/ Bye Bye to Auction Street/ Bye Bye too many sold/ Bye Bye too many beat
> They makin' niggahs extinct/
> too many drugs in the jail meat/
> Chickenheads ain't comin' home to roost/ And Welfare man stopped sellin' Juicy Juice/
> Ain't gone have nobody to play with afterwhile/ . . . while . . . while
> Shit! I done got off my rhyme.
> *(COOKIE looks out into at the audience.)*
> COOKIE *(cont.)*
> Remember when the candylady used to live on the Seventh

St. side of the complex? You could get them pink cheweys for two cents a dollop. You can't buy shit for two cents no mo. E'erthang cost nearbout a dollar. Inflation. Fuck Bush! Remember when we use to play Curbball? Object of the game: you had to stand on yo' porch and hit the curb of yo' neighbors porch with a ball. If you hit they curb, you got a point. If it bounced back and hit yours, you got a double. Hell, yeah! I was the queen of mutha-fuckin' curbball. Wun't nobody betta than me. Or how 'bout when folks'll be outside playin' "Hide the Belt"? You'd take yo' mama's most favoritist belt she whip you wit and somebody like, Ray-Ray or Peaches, would go behind the complex and hide it. When they fount it, e'erbody would break for the base cause whoever got the belt could beat the shit out of e'erbody! Base'll be somebody porch that had a couch on it so you could sit down and catch yo breath after runnin' so hard. I still got welts til' this day. I couldn't run for shit. Us project kids cleverah than a muthafucka, maine. Mmph, mmph, mmph them was the days. Fo' it got bad. I mean Hurt Village always been bad, but it done got *bad-bad*, like you-betta-move-yo-Big-Mama-out-these-muthafuckin-projects-fo-she-get-gang-raped-robbed-and-murdered-by-her-Gangsta Disciple crack head son bad. Children can't even go outside to play no more. I'n played Curb-ball in I don't know how long. They done already moved a lota folk out. We the last ones. That why Big Mama been bein cheap. She been savin' up her scrilla for a minute for when we move to our new house. Oooooo, Big Mama know she been bein' cheap as hell. Memphis be hot as a muthafucka in the summer and she don't be lettin' a niggah turn on the air conditioner for mo' than 15 minutes at a time. Always yakkin' "You gone run up the light bill." She'en even have to pay for 'lectricity! They give that shit to us for free! But I guess po' folk always gotsta be savin' they scrilla. Like take Dawn dishwashin' liquid for instance. That's stuff the shit, ain't it? It's for more than just dishes. It body wash, washin' detergent, Windex, bubble bath, Barbie shampoo . . . Yeah, maine. Folks round here so po' we can't even afford the r at the end. Project niggahs have to think fast, cry later. Livin' o'er here can try you sometimes. I done had fun though. But I'm 13, and I'm a grown ass woman now.

THE INVITATION

Brian Parks

Comic
Marian, fifty to sixty

Marian is mocking her husband David's liberal offer to host a dinner party for some homeless people. The monologue references the fact that David has had a novel he wrote rejected by the publishing house he works for. She is speaking to both David and three other dinner guests.

MARIAN: It's a bit cruel, don't you think?
(indicating the people at the table)
Inviting your best friends to an event they in no way wish to attend? Have the party! But how does one top it next year? Perhaps with an *asylum* theme! What could be more lively than a cocktail party for the *insane*? The ebb and flow of conversation. About the brilliant Farsi spoken by the voices in their head. How the South would have won the Civil War if they'd gotten a little more of *that promised help* from the sea gods. I can see them all mingling, holding their cocktails with one hand, their pants up with their other. A couple meets-cute, then sneaks to the bedroom and jams hands into each other's crusty privates, discovering, in the process, small crawly creatures previously unknown to entomologists! And the fashions! What are the hem lines this year in the gutter? The make-up—*soot* really brings out the cheekbones! What kind of ring does Tiffany design for the finger normally reserved for picking cat-food out from between molars? The party will be massive on the gossip pages! "Last Friday, noted editor David Northrup was the proud host of a *non*-book party for his *not*-printed literary masterpiece, an event celebrated with a strongly aromatic crowd of his *un*-published peers, unless *the police blotter* counts as a *print run*." Ah, that phantom called art! If you

want to write, write something *useful*. Miscarriage condolence cards! A huge, untapped market! "Our sympathies on your half-formed loss."

Information on this playwright may be found at
www.smithandkraus.com. Click on the AUTHORS tab.

KISSING SID JAMES

Robert Farquhar

Comic
Crystal, thirties

> *Crystal has agreed to go with Eddie to a British seaside resort for the weekend, even though it's basically only their second date. Eddie is totally clueless about how to please a woman, so Crystal has suggested that they fantasy-role play. She's asked him to start by telling her who his dream woman is. After thinking this over, he tells her "Betty Rubble." Well, that isn't going to get the home fires burning, so Crystal takes the bull by the horns, so to speak, and tells him that her ultimate fantasy is to have torrid sex with Sir Sean Connery.*

CRYSTAL: Oh yes. Sean Connery. I'd be resting on my bed at home. And I'd have put on clean sheets and I'd have lit loads of candles and I'd have just had a nice long bath. And the pillows would be all puffed up, and I'd be waiting. I would be waiting in a state of complete and utter openness. And I'd be wearing a pair of black stockings, and a flimsy see-thru nightie thing. And I'd be waiting, anticipating, and I'd be watching the telly, some sexy foreign thing. And then the door would slowly edge open, and this big male masculine shadow would just sort of emerge. And it would be him. And he'd be all tanned and mysterious and brooding. And he'd reach over and click the telly off. And then he'd stroll round the room, looking at me. Just looking at me. Looking at me all over. Undressing me mentally. And then he'd make his move, and I'd be engulfed by his big powerful arms. And we'd kiss. And oh boy does he know to kiss. And I can smell him. Oh yes, he smells of, of pure Sean Connery. And then he'd lean back, and he'd rip off my flimsy see-thru nightie as easy, as easy as, pulling a curtain. And then he'd start to unbutton his shirt, and as he did that, I'd kneel down, and I'd undo his belt, and I'd gently begin to ease off, oh yes, and then underneath . . .

(CRYSTAL is getting into this more and more.)

Right, so he's naked. And I'm naked. Apart from my stockings. I've still got those on. And I want him. I want him like nothing else, and then he takes me. Oh God he takes me Like some sort of silent deadly panther. And we do it. We do it. Every way possible. We even invent a few positions. And it just goes on. On and on all night. For hours and hours, and he doesn't say anything, just every now and then he mumbles my name, and I think I didn't know it was possible to feel all this, to feel this close to someone, to know somebody so intimately. And then just as the sun is beginning to rise, and the first few rays of the virgin day are filtering into our temple of love, we reach, simultaneously, the most glorious and earth-shattering orgasm. Comparable only to a volcano. And we both collapse, like marathon runners crossing the tape, and he holds me, and he whispers my name, and I fall asleep. And I have a beautiful dream, and then, when I wake up, and he's gone. But it doesn't matter because I am happy, and I am fulfilled, and I know that I am the most special woman in the world.

Information on this playwright may be found at www.smithandkraus.com. Click on the AUTHORS tab.

LIDLESS

Frances Ya-Chu Cowhig

Dramatic
Alice, twenty-five

> *Alice is an interrogator at Guantanamo Bay prison. She is*
> *a tactic called 'Invasion of Space by a Female' in which the*
> *threat of female sexuality is used to break down a Muslim*
> *man suspected of being a terrorist.*

ALICE: Hey now. For a second there, with the light on you
like that, you looked like my Lucas. Call me overworked
and underfucked, but from where I'm standing, ya'll could
be cousins.
(beat)
I'm touching myself. My fingers trail up my thigh as I think
of all our bodies could do. I could sink onto your hard, hot
cock. I could bury my face in your neck. You could hold
me. You could move me. You could help me find light and
redemption and peace. What's the matter, Mo? Is the great
Islamic sword too weary to rise today?
(beat)
Holy mother. Looks like I found your sweet spot. Right here.
An inch beneath your left ear. Jesus. I could hang Old Glory
on that pole. I've been wasting my time on white boys. It
appears those rumors about Asian men are lies your ladies
tell to keep you to themselves. Selfish bitches. Now. What
are we going to do about that boner?
(Alice flinches. She wipes invisible spit off her face.)
Now, now. The only spittin' allowed is the kind that comes
from down there. Besides. You like this. Our heads and
hearts try to trick us, but our bodies never lie. Roll with
me, baby. Don't fight. Give it up, sweet pea. Stop your
prayin'. If Allah was in Gitmo, we'd have him in solitary,
so he wouldn't be able to hear you anyway.
(beat)
I forgot to tell you, I'm bleeding, and there's nothing shield-

ing you from my twenty-five-year-old cunt, just red, red, red, stainin' skin already caked pus white and blue with bruises, making you the color of the flag I've sworn to protect. I've read about your hell. Your silence condemns you to that furnace fueled by the flesh of men, where walls are fire, smoke's the only shade, and the only beverage is the blood bubbling through your burning skin. Stay silent and my blood will damn your veins, so you better hope to Allah there's no such thing as eternity.

(Alice takes off her shirt, revealing a lacy red push-up bra.)

Last chance.

Love And Marriage And All That Stuff

Jan Forster

Comic
Sherry, early twenties

Sherry is standing outside City Hall, about to go and get married, when she tells her husband to be, Bobby, something she's never told him before.

SHERRY: Bobby, there's just one or two little things I'd like to mention before we go in there . . . after all, marriage is forever and two people who have found themselves in this situation should know every last detail about each other, don't you agree? You can tell me all your quirks, but let me go first, because I'm a little nervous. And I'm only closing my eyes while I share this with you because if I look at you while I say it, it'll never get said, so no interruptions . . . okay? Well . . . you know how you can sshhh me with a kiss when I get going. Anyway, Bobby, I think you should know . . . I get these headaches. Not big ones . . . little ones . . . little migraines. They just sneak up on me when I least expect it and they can hang on for days, the buggers. I mention this only because they can sometimes interfere with . . . you know . . . things . . . oh, you know. My shrink says I'm repressing some—oh, I never mentioned a shrink, did I? Well . . . a few years ago . . . oh, it's nothing, really . . . well . . . a few years ago I had a little tiny, itty, bitty nothing—and I mean nothing—breakdown. It was nothing. I'm fine and I don't know what everybody's so worried about! I spent about six months in a sanitarium—and what the hell, I had nothing important going on in my life at the time anyway— it was like a country club, Bobby. I mean, I laugh about it now. Anyway . . . as I was saying about my shrink . . . . He thinks I'm—oh, it's ridiculous . . . most of what he says is a lot of horse manure but daddy pays him a hundred and fifty an hour so he gets to be right. I keep threatening to get rid of him but he's number twenty-two and daddy says a hundred and fifty's a bargain. Well, I don't care what that quack says, if there's anything that can cure a headache it's a big fat shopping spree at Bloomingdale's or Saks . . . oh, I know that's a nothing thing to you, Bobby . . . though I do tend to go a wee bit overboard with my charge cards . . . which is why I think it might be a good idea to reconsider daddy's offer to bring you into the business, Bobby. Daddy says I'm the most expensive child he's ever known, and if daddy with all his money says that, what chance do we have without his help? I know how much you like to be your own man, Bobby, but you'll see how reasonable daddy can be once he knows you're on his side . . . which is why I want you to promise me that you'll always, always—like everyone in my family—vote Republican, Bobby, and end this silly rebellious stand of yours like registering as an independent. You would be an absolute saint in daddy's eyes and it would be good practice for when the children arrive. When my little boy and girl enter this world—and I want you to promise me we'll keep trying in that department till we get it right—when they arrive I want them to have a very stable family background . . . there's nothing that confuses children more than constant bickering among family members—God knows, look what happened to me—

(short pause)

and this sex thing, Bob? All I can say is, thank God we're getting married so I don't have to fake it anymore. Well, Bobby . . . these are just a few of the things that are important to me. I'm ready to take the plunge now!

(Sherry nervously opens her eyes and looks around slowly, calling out.)

Bobby? . . . Bobby? . . . Bobby?

Information on this playwright may be found at www.smithandkraus.com. Click on the AUTHORS tab.

LUCK OF THE IRISH

Kirsten Greenidge

Dramatic
Nessa, thirty, African American

Nessa is speaking to Rich, her sister's husband, late thirties, that she did not get the promotion she'd hoped for at work.

NESSA: I just like coming over. I like lying here. I lie here on the grass and pretend. It's stupid. . . I . . . pretend . . . that I've been here all day. I pretend I'm exhausted 'cause I spent the morning riding bikes with the kids. I pretend Hannah and me made lunch and then dinner and then sat out here in the lawn chairs sipping wine while the kids run through that field. I pretend. My mom taught us to be kinda on guard, right? I guess it's not Hannah's fault she's just like that in general now. I guess everyone does it eventually. After high school, after college, after your first job when the blonde guy you started as an intern with gets promoted and you can't bond over the five dollar Indian lunch buffet cause all of a sudden he has enough to go to P.F. Chang's or something. Everyone does it, I guess. It's what makes you an adult, I think. It's what makes you stop making mix tapes and start sending e cards.
(pause)
I didn't get that promotion. Craig? Who spends half his day tending a virtual farm on Facebook? He got it. He asked for it and he got it and I don't think I could even ask my boss for permission to go to the bathroom, never mind a raise. I'd just hold and it hope for the best. Craig can't stop talking about P.F. Chang's. I want to rip his throat out. I sit next to him and I swear I smell something very old on the sleeves of his shirts, on the curves of his cuffs. Craig's mothy and sweaty but sweet with ease, I smell him and I smell his ease and I don't have that I don't know that I can't taste that or touch that or know that and and I want to rip his throat out. I want to reach down into his neck and strip out, claw out

every last piece of anything that makes him speak and talk with all that fucking ease.

MAPLE AND VINE

Jordan Harrison

Comic
Ellen, thirties to early forties

> *Ellen and her husband live in a community of reenactors*
> *called the Society of Dynamic Obsolescence, in which ev-*
> *eryone lives as if they are in the 1950s. She speaks to us*
> *as if we are the newest recruits of the society. She smokes,*
> *wonderfully.*

ELLEN: Here are some things you've never heard of:
Hummus.
Baba Ganoush.
Falafel.
Focaccia.
Ciabatta
Whole grain bread.
(She raises her eyebrows significantly: "Yes, not even whole-
grain bread.")
Portobello mushrooms
Shiitake mushrooms
Chipotle peppers
Chipotle anything.
Jamaican Jerk.
Miso.
Sushi.
That one is hard for me.
But I do without.
You'll do without too.
Gruyere
Manchego
Parmiggiano Reggiano – the parmesan in a can is all right.
No Kalamata olives
No pine nuts
No pesto
No *Lattes.*

That's hard for a lot of people.
What you get
Is salt.
You get pepper.
Mayonnaise. Mustard.
You get dried oregano. Basil.
Bay leaves.
Paprika, if you want a little kick.
Sanka.
It's a relief, the limitations. You'll find that it's a relief.
It may be hard to maintain a vegetarian lifestyle. Some people have tried. You're always welcome to try, if it coincides with the rest of your Dossier. For instance, it might coincide with the Dossier of a beatnik English professor Ð but if you're taking on the identity of an oil man or an ad executive, it would be pretty disruptive not to have steak and a martini for lunch. Disrupting means you're not period-appropriate.
One question we get a lot is health concerns.
"Do I *have* to smoke?"
"Do I *have* to drink?"
"Do I *have* to eat hot fudge sundaes."
Of course , we can't ask for more commitment than you're willing to give. But we think you will get much more out of the experience with total commitment, total authenticity.
What's a little hypertension if you're happy?

Information on this playwright may be found at www.smithandkraus.com. Click on the AUTHORS tab.

Milk Like Sugar

Kirsten Greenidge

Dramatic
Keera, sixteen, African American

Keera is speaking to Annie, her friend who is also 16, finally telling her the truth about her family, which is not as holy as she has let on.

KEERA: The truth. The truth is: every second of every day I pray to be someone else, anyone else, but me, for even just a moment. Eventhough I am good. I am, I am so. Good. I. Visit my father every week. Don't got no one to take me so I take the Greyhound. I go every week. Honor thy father and thy mother: that thy days may be long upon the land which the Lord thy God giveth thee. I go every week even though he got on that orange jump suit. And I got to talk to him behind glass through a phone I know he found his way. He the one, in his letters, start telling me about the Word. Start telling me to read my Bible. That when I started in going to church, after my Dad dy went away. My mom ain't never found her way. She plays the coin slots down Foxwoods. Takes her whole paycheck down Foxwoods. She don't remember my gym clothes. She barely remember what grade I'm on. But. Pastor say his home always open, long as my heart stay pure and I work for the Lord and that what my texts be doin'. I doing the work of the Lord. I deserve tablecloths and real forks and real spoons.
(beat)
I deserve them. I deserve them. I should be wearing satin, I should be shielded, I should be playing Yahtzee, I should, I should, I. I.
(a recovery)
This is vanity, Keera. This is a sin, Keera, this is sin, Keera, this is sin, this is sin, this is—

MILK LIKE SUGAR

Kirsten Greenidge

Dramatic
Talisha, sixteen, African American

Talisha tells her friend Annie how she got her new phone.

TALISHA: Older guys just like things certain ways is all. Like today he take me to the mall tell me pick whatever phone I like, right? I look in the case and my face get hot, right? I don't want to pick something too much, right? I point to one and he say naw, baby, who you think I am some kinda of chump? Pick again. This time I be sweatin' right? Like I can feel sweat dripping down the back my shirt, right? So I pick again. See he got all his boys with him and he don't want me make him look like he some broke ass scrub in front of them can't afford a nice phone. So he turn to one of them, and he say, she must think I'm a chump, shit. And his boy laugh loud right. And then all them start laughing loud and my guy started to get mad right, like real angry, and then he say, he say T who the hell you been with that make you feel you don't deserve best, right? And one of his boys says well she ain't been with me yet, and I know I gotta answer right the next time and my guy says Now you look in that case baby girl and you tell me which you want. I so, I so don't want to get it wrong again so I look in and I pick this and he say that my baby girl. And I stop sweatin cause I did it right for him. The tones, the minutes, the apps is all unlimited I can pick all I want. You got Malik on a string like this?

The Motherfu**ker With the Hat

Stephen Adly Guirgis

Seriocomic
Veronica, twenties

> *Veronica's boyfriend Jackie has flipped out when he discovered a man's hat in their room in a transient hotel. He is convinced she is having sex with the guy whose hat it is (of course, she is ...). Veronica denies it and tries to mollify him.*

VERONICA: Callate! Look, let's just go there, to the pie place, and we'll have, like, some pie, and we'll just, like, talk, or not even talk, we'll just eat pie first and be. And after that, we'll talk. You have got this wrong, Jackie. You're so far out of line you're like in Zimbabwe or some shit, but I think maybe cooler heads could prevail on both our parts at the pie place, so let's just go there. I'm willing to do that. I'm willing to put the ghetto on hold and eat some fuckin' pie with you, if you're willing to entertain the notion that you're a fuckin' retard ex-con who almost blew it cuz you got an imagination like—I dunno—Dr. fuckin' Seuss an shit. Okay? Look at me: I didn't fuck no body. Jackie, you know how I am. You know I'm a little fuckin' crazy just like you're a little fuckin' crazy, and you know I'd rather spit on a nun's cunt than give a fuckin' inch when I been wronged. I been wronged here. You wronged me. Really, really fuckin' badly. But I will concede to you—and it ain't a small concession—that I love your ass. And I'll kick a 3-legged kitten down a flight of fuckin' stairs rather than say some shit like I love you. You know that. So let's go get some fuckin' pie before someone here says something that can't be changed. Okay?

Information on this playwright may be found at www.smithandkraus.com. Click on the AUTHORS tab.

THE MOUNTAINTOP

Katori Hall

Dramatic
Camae, twenties, African American

> *The Mountaintop takes place in Dr. Martin Luther's King's room at the Lorraine Motel in Memphis on the night before he was assassinated. Dr. King has called down to the front desk and asked for some coffee, which has been brought to him by Camae, a maid. King, who's lonely and more than a little attracted to Camae, has asked her to stay awhile and keep him company. Here, Camae reveals to Dr. King who she really is.*

CAMAE: You perfect? Then why should I be? Honey, I've robbed. I've lied. I've cheated. I've failed. I've cursed. But what I'm ashamed of most is I've hated. Hated myself. Sacrificed my flesh so that others might feel whole again. I thought it was my duty. All that I had to offer this world. What else was a poor black woman, the mule of the world, here for? Last night, in the back of a alley I breathed my last breath. A man clasped his hands like a necklace 'round my throat. I stared into his big blue eyes, as my breath got ragged and raw, and I saw the Hell this old world had put him through . The time he saw his father hang a man. The time he saw his mother raped. I felt so sorry for him. I saw what the world had done to him, and I still couldn't forgive. I hated him for stealing my breath. When I passed on to the other side, God—ooooo, she is more gorgeous than me. She the color of midnight and her eyes are brighter than the stars. Her hair . . . well . . . just you wait til you see her hair—God stood there before me. With this look on her face. I just knowed she was just soooo disappointed in me. I was just a' cryin' weepin' at her feet. Beggin' her not to throw me down. All that sinnin'. All that grime on my soul. All that hatred in my heart. But then I looked up and saw that She was smilin' down at me. She opened her mouth, and silence came out. But I heard her loud and clear. "I got a special task for you and if you complete it, all your sins will be washed away." I opened my file. And I saw my task was you. What could little old me, give to big old you? I thought you was gone be perfect. Well, you ain't, but then you are. You have the biggest heart I done ever known. You have the strength to love those who could never love you back. If I had just a small fraction of the love you have for this world, then maybe, just maybe I could become half the angel you are.

THE MOUNTAINTOP

Katori Hall

Seriocomic
Camae, twenties, African American

> *The Mountaintop takes place in Dr. Martin Luther's King's
> room at the Lorraine Motel in Memphis on the night before
> he was assassinated. Dr. King has called down to the front
> desk and asked for some coffee, which has been brought to
> him by Camae, a maid. King, who's lonely and more than a
> little attracted to Camae, has asked her to stay awhile and
> keep him company. Here, he has asked her what she would
> preach if she were in his pulpit.*

CAMAE: *(with a "King" voice)* Chuuch! We have gathered
here today to deal with a serious issue. It is an issue of
great paponderance—you like that?—Paponderance! It is
a matter of importance more serious than my overgrown
mustache: *HOW do we deal with the white man?* I have
told you that the white man is our brother. And he should
be treated as such. We touch our brother with the softest
of hands. We greet our brothers with the widest of smiles.
We give our brother food when he is hungry. But it is hard
to do this when our brother beats his fist upon our flesh.
When he greets us with "Nigger" and "Go back to Africa,"
when he punches us in our bellies swelling with hunger.
Abel was slain by his brother Cain and just like the Biblical
times, today the white man is killing his Negro brethren,
shackling his hands, keeping us from rising to the stars we
are booooouuuuuund to occupy. We have walked. Our feet
swelling with each step. We have been drowned by hoses.
Our dreams being washed away. We have been bitten by
dogs. Our skin forever scarred by hatred at its height. Our
Godly crowns have been turned into ashtrays for white men
at lunch counters all across the South. To this I say, my
brethren, a new day is coming. I'm sick and tired of being
sick and tired, and today is the day that I tell you to KILL

the white man! *(sotto voice)* But not with your hands. Not with your guns. But with your miiiiiiind! *(back to regular voice)*. We are fighting to sit at the same counter, but WHY, my brothers and sisters? We should build our own counters. Our own restaurants. Our own neighborhoods. Our own schools. The white man ain't got nothin' I want. Fuck the white man! FUCK the white man! I say, FUCK 'em! *(pause)* I AM SO SORRY! Preacher, Kang. Ooooooo. I just can't control my mouth.

Paraffin—(from The Hallway Trilogy)

Adam Rapp

Seriocomic
Dena, thirties

> *Dena is talking to a friend about the many permutations that can occur in one's life-path.*

DENA: And so can bad things, but that's my point. We get so stuck in our lives. I've been working at the same publishing company for eight years. I walk the same route to work. I take the elevator to the same floor, talk to the same agents on the phone, attend the same boring editorial meetings. I eat my lunch at roughly the same time every day. On Saturdays I go to Film Forum or to a play at Lincoln Center and I have Sunday brunch with a sociable articulate friend whose outfit often equals his or her capacity to charm and then I usually come over here and spend a few hours with Margo complaining about all of it and nothing really changes. I mean everyone here's probably been through some cursory existential philosophy class. We've studied our bit of Sartre and Kierkegaard and we've read William Barrett and talked about action and inaction and what it means to be alive and how most of us wind up middle-aged zombies, etcetera, etcetera, but if you really stop to think about it—if you really consider the possibility, isn't it amazing how, on a candlelit night without the comfort of cable television or the Internet or your porn collection, or your favorite halogen lamp, whathaveyou, isn't it amazing how one irrational choice could change your life? Let's say I did go into Kevin's apartment and fuck his brains out. Any number of things could happen. I could start shrieking for joy. I could get vertigo. I could freak out and curl into a ball. I could have an Olympic orgasm. I could spontaneously get my period. I could get a fucking yeast infection and wind up spooning yogurt into my vagina! I could have multiple outerbody, extraterrestrial orgasms till my ears bled and realize I've met my soul mate. We could fall in love. The possibilities are endless.

Information on this playwright may be found at www.smithandkraus.com. Click on the AUTHORS tab.

PONZI

Elaine Romero

Dramatic
Catherine, forties

At a party, Catherine, a rich heiress who recently lost her father, flirts with Bryce. Bryce is more recent to his fortune. He has invested his money with a financial manager named Jack. Catherine has formed a lot of opinions about money that she learned from her father. She uses her knowledge to seduce Bryce.

CATHERINE: Money isn't real. There used to be the gold standard. And every U.S. dollar was backed by something significant. This many dollars in your pocket represented this many gold bars in Fort Knox. Do you know what happened? President Nixon nixed any relationship between gold and the U.S. dollar. And he claimed he was not a crook. August 15th 1971. A day that will be remembered in infamy. My dad used to cite it as if it were the official Declaration of Destabilization. The death knell that only people who were paying attention ever heard. The U.S. goes off the gold standard. We start printing paper money, backed by nothing. A house of cards waiting to collapse. In debt to a country we don't even like. A nation torn between our ethics and our greed. And Social Security? One big Ponzi scheme. Money's not backed by anything anymore. Not even gold. There's this game the adults used to play. With their money. Fifty thousand dollars each. That was a sizable fortune back then. And one time, I was hanging out with my parents, and we got invited to the "airplane party." And the whole gig was that people, from the neighborhood, lined up like they were in airplane seats. The first person, the pilot, got 7 friends to give him $50,000, and then they got 7 friends to give them the same. You know the deal. Everybody's going to get rich. Good things come to those who wait. And they asked their friends because that's how it worked. I was something like seven years old, or ten, nothing short of nine, and I knew intuitively that somebody was going to get screwed. Somebody was going to be caught holding the airplane bag. I looked at the people in those seats. These young couples who already lived a mile from the beach and they just wanted more. Because a lot of cash, and 99.9% more than the rest of the world, sometimes feels insufficient. And there's this pregnant woman with bleached blonde hair. And she's sitting with her husband and they're smiling. Like they're making this stellar investment for their unborn child. Even though some people might say they deserved what they had coming. I cried inside. I knew they were going to lose their $50,000. A veritable fortune. I knew that they were going to fight over it. Maybe divorce over it. And that they were going to regret this choice for the rest of their lives. And that she was going to blame him, and he was going to blame her, and that they weren't even going to remember why they ultimately made the decision. Because it was made by somebody else. The collective. The group. If you can find your way around things in a way that others haven't, if you can outsmart the rest of everybody, you might be a real winner. For once. You might finally be on top—the place you know you deserve. To be. And then later I heard that it was only the people at the front of the plane that survived.

(laughs ironically)

Nothing like real plane crashes. The rest of them "lost their shirts," as my father liked to say. Because they wanted more. I decided I would never be one of those people who got too far in the back of the plane.

Information on this playwright may be found at www.smithandkraus.com. Click on the AUTHORS tab.

THE RELEASE OF A LIVE PERFORMANCE

Sherry Kramer

Seriocomic
Nell, twenties to early thirties

A year ago, Nell fell in love with a man she spent one night with, and she doesn't know how to fall out of love with him. Everything in the world—including other men—reminds her of him, so she's spent the year remembering him in some very horizontal ways, with a different man every night. William Blake says, "the desire suppressed is no true desire." But her older sister Coco, a married, middle of the road, mother-of-two, doesn't care if it's true or not. She's come back to Texas to rescue Nell from her desire. Nell tries to tell Coco what it's like to be in the center of a world made out of longing.

NELL: Everything I see, everything I touch—
 (She rubes her neck.)
Lord, Lord, He's got a nape of the neck!
(She points at a chair.)
And chair! Damn if he doesn't have a chair too! Jesusus, what a miracle! Swing low, sweet chair-i-o-t.
(She tumbles onto the floor.)
And he's got a floor. Got a rug too, I'll bet.
(Runs her fingers through the rug)
Got 100,000 closely threaded machine loomed fibers. I think about them. I think about him.
(She crawls around on the floor.)
He's got couch legs. Table bases.
(She is at the door.)
Doors. Windows.
(Stands and looks outside the window)
Drives. Outside of his house he's got—
(pause)
—an outside.
(She touches the shirt she's wearing.)
He's got a shirt. He's got all kinds of them. He puts them

on. He takes them off. Sometimes I see shirts, and I want to see hundreds of 'em. I want to see them around me, in front of me, behind me, back through all recorded time. At times like that, I can't help myself. I jump in the car and drive to Neiman Marcus—the Men's Department. I run inside and I want to scream SHIRTS! ALL THESE SHIRTS COULD BE HIS SHIRTS! He could wear every shirt in the store. Oh Lord should you see me in Neiman Marcus. I've almost died there. Twice I've almost just pulled down a display on top of me and died. The fucking wonder of it all, Coco—that's what I'm talking about! It's the miracle of shirts! Like the famous shroud of Turin. I see him there. In every one of them. And when I walk into Neiman Marcus they can't tell. I look like a perfectly normal person—no one can tell! And boy do I love walking down the street, mingling with all those damn normal people—riding the same buses, sitting at the same luncheonettes, eating the same tasteless food. How I'd love it, someday at the luncheonette, some one day when everybody is eating the same runny mashed potatoes, the same dry turkey slice, how I'd love to stand up some one day and scream "You poor slobs! You poor, ordinary himless slobs! You're eating this shit but I'm thinking of him!"

Information on this playwright may be found at
www.smithandkraus.com. Click on the AUTHORS tab.

THE RELEASE OF A LIVE PERFORMANCE

Sherry Kramer

Seriocomic
Nell, twenties to early thirties

A year ago, Nell fell in love with a man she spent one night with, and she doesn't know how to fall out of love with him. Everything in the world—including other men—reminds her of him, so she's spent the year remembering him in some very horizontal ways, with a different man every night. William Blake says, "the desire suppressed is no true desire." But her older sister Coco, a married, middle of the road, mother-of-two, doesn't care if it's true or not. She's come back to Texas to rescue Nell from her desire. Nell tries to tell Coco what it's like to be in the center of a world made out of longing.

NELL: Here's what I didn't tell you: There's no way back. There isn't anything I can do that doesn't make me think of him and when I think of him there's nothing left worth doing. Nothing. For awhile I thought I had it licked. I took care of myself. I did things right. I felt the pleasure of doing things right. Things got very right for awhile around here—the house was very clean and there was a lot of gourmet eating going on and I was to work on time and my bank balance was a piece of anal retentive art. Things got very right and I felt the pleasure of it, felt it fully, one day, for about thirty seconds. That was my mistake. My first, last, and always mistake. My always. I can make this chair—if I try very hard—I can make this ordinary chair not remind me of him. It's an act of the magic of hard work, but I'm not afraid of hard work. It can be done and I can do it. I can hard work systematically across this room like a minesweeper, disengaging every snap, crackle and pop. But I can't break the hold—*(She touches her heart.)*—in here. You walked into this house. You know—you must know—how warm and good it feels to have you walk into this house. And everything it feels like is him.

Information on this playwright may be found at www.smithandkraus.com. Click on the AUTHORS tab.

THE RELEASE OF A LIVE PERFORMANCE

Sherry Kramer

Seriocomic
Nell, twenties to early thirties

> *A year ago, Nell fell in love with a man she spent one night with, and she doesn't know how to fall out of love with him. Everything in the world—including other men—reminds her of him, so she's spent the year remembering him in some very horizontal ways, with a different man every night. William Blake says, "the desire suppressed is no true desire." But her older sister Coco, a married, middle of the road, mother-of-two, doesn't care if it's true or not. She's come back to Texas to rescue Nell from her desire. What Coco hadn't planned on was how strong the gravity of her sister's world would be. She asks Nell to help her understand what it feels like. Nell tells Coco to lie down on the floor on her back, and close her eyes.*

NELL: Now. They say to start with a swimming pool. I want you to understand that somebody else, they'd start you off with a swimming pool. Not me. I mean, sure, it's clear and blue, but it's not real water, you know? It's used water. And besides, the neighbor's kids have been pissing in it. That's why I prefer the Aegean Sea. Ready? Here we go.
(Softly)
Imagine that you are lying on the fine, white sand on the shore of the Aegean Sea. It is a clear . . . warm . . . bright summer day. The Aegean's a sea you can see all in one place. It doesn't move around a lot like the big 7 do. And it's warm. All that land around it makes it warm. Imagine doing it with the Arctic Ocean—you're talking icebergs, you're talking chunks of dirty gray ice the size of Manhattan. The Aegean Sea is more green than blue, they say—I've never seen it. I suppose there are more things in a sea than there are in swimming pools—tuna and sharks and lots of microscopic swimming things—but I just can't picture doing it with a

concrete, chlorinated pool. What would be the point? Are you relaxed now? That little talk was supposed to relax you. Get you primed. Imagine you are lying on your back on the fine, hard white sand on the shore of the Aegean Sea. You are looking up at the sky. It is more blue than any blue you have ever seen. You part your legs slightly. They open onto the bright, clear water. You hear the sound of the waves, breaking gently. You close your eyes. You draw in, with something inside you. It takes a moment or two, but gradually the water begins flowing up between your legs. The movement of the water feels—it feels—full. Whatever it is between your legs can suck, can pull, you suck and pull with. The water rushes in, past every soft, smooth place inside you. By now you know for sure where it is inside you that can suck and pull. By now you know how good it feels. By now you are ready to stop. Already ten's of thousands of gallons have emptied into you. The level of the Aegean Sea, if you looked—but you don't look, you keep your eyes closed, you keep on sucking in—by now the level of the water is two, then five, then twenty feet lower, if you looked you'd see the great Aegean Sea shrinking, you'd see it funneling, disappearing into you, and you'd stop. But you don't stop. You'd see the slime and rock exposed banks, the naked bottom of the sea, the countless water creatures, gasping in the air, and you'd stop. You can't stop. You keep on, sucking in and in. And it feels wonderful, and it feels full and it will never fill you. Never.

Information on this playwright may be found at
www.smithandkraus.com. Click on the AUTHORS tab.

ROGER AND VANESSA

Brett C. Leonard

Dramatic
Vanessa, thirties

Vanessa discusses her Uncle Charlie with Roger. She hopes Roger doesn't end up going down the same road.

VANESSA: When you was locked up. I thought maybe . . . I dunno. Like you wouldn't get out maybe. Or when you did, you'd just get locked up again. I dunno. No money. Didn't wanna really tell no one. I didn't know what ta do. A fucked up dirty clinic, ya know? A public fuckin'—I didn't know. With the tempers. Our fighting. Your drinking. An' they put me on this table. This cold table, with this paper sheet crinklin' underneath me. An' this bitch, baby. This fuckin' nurse. The doctor's 'bout ready ta stick this fuckin' vacuum shit up in me, my legs in these cold stirrups. Ready ta suck a child outta me. Our child. This bitch's holdin' my hand, sayin' "Don't worry—I've had three a these things. Relax an' ya won't feel a thing." *(beat)* Don't go away again, okay? Promise me you won't go anywhere. Promise me. I didn't like it when you were gone. When I was growin' up, I had this Uncle Charlie. It was my mother, my grandmother, my brothers an' sisters, my aunt Marisol, my cousins Eva an' Angela, an' Felix an' Emilio, an' my cousin Ana Marie. An' my Uncle Charlie. In a five room no more'n maybe about ten blocks from here. My Uncle Charlie sat around wearin' long-john thermal underwear's no matter what the weather. An' he wore these blue-tinted swimmer's goggles. Blue-tinted swimmer's goggles an' 'is long-johns. He was this old gangster who sat around an' smoked cigars all day an' night. He wore the swimmer's goggles cuz he said the smoke bothered his eyes. An' he didn't really like ta say much either—'cept for maybe ta yell at us, or curse at us for whatever. An' these other men would always be comin' in an' out at all kinda hours an' stuff. Bringin' stacks a money with 'em. Bottles a' booze with no labels. Lotta pills. Drugs. They were mostly nice, mostly—tellin' jokes, sometimes bringin' me an' my cousins little gifts, chocolate candies. Uncle Charlie was never nice. Not that I remember. An' I mostly jus' stayed away from'm mosta the time. I brought'm his food when he wanted, folded his towels, fluffed his pillows. But mostly—mostly I jus' stayed away. An' I KNEW. .I KNEW he was gonna kill me someday. I knew it. So I started writin' these little notes that said . . . "It was Uncle Charlie that did it. It was Uncle Charlie that killed me." An' I put 'em everywhere. I hid 'em under the lamps, inside the cookbooks. Under the bathmat in the bathroom. Everywhere. Then one day . . . Uncle Charlie jus' never got off 'is E-Z chair ta go take 'is nap. Every day, two a'clock sharp, every day he'd go an' take his daily nap. But this day he never left his E-Z chair. An' no one wanted ta ask'm why not cuz Uncle Charlie didn't like people askin' a lotta much a anything. Come dinner time, I wen' ta bring'm 'is food. "Uncle Charlie," I said. "Uncle Charlie. Uncle Charlie, your food is ready." He didn't say nothin' back. He didn't even move. He jus' stayed there sittin in one position. The doctors said he musta had some sorta' heart attack or stroke or somethin'. At the funeral he was wearin' a suit my aunt Marisol musta bought for'm new, 'cause I never saw'm in no suit before. He looked handsome in that new brown suit but, I dunno . . . I think he woulda liked it better with 'is goggles an' 'is long-johns, I think. But the thing is . . . I never remembered seein' 'is eyes before then. Before seein' 'em when I found him in the E-Z chair—I found him an', an' I lifted up his goggles—an' his eyes were wide open. They were nice ta look at. 'An I remember I jus' stood there starin' at'm an' 'is nice eyes. For the longest time. I jus' stared at his eyes. An' then I felt BAD about the notes I wrote. An' I couldn't stop crying. Crying like I never remembered cryin' before. When we got home after the funeral, I remember thinkin' it was too bad they hadda sew 'is eyes up in the coffin, you know, for the parting glance. I wished I coulda seen' em again. An' I bet a lotta other people woulda liked that too. I couldn't sleep that night an' I got up an' went an' looked under the lamps, but didn't find no notes. Not under any of 'em. Same with inside the cookbooks, an' under the bathmat, an' behind the soup cans. None of 'em were left anywhere I put 'em. An' one day when I was like some'n like fourteen or fifteen, five-six years after Uncle Charlie died—I was goin' through a box a drawings an' finger paintings an' old collages an' stuff I'd been savin' in a box in the closet since elementary school an', an' I found this note. Mixed in with all a my stuff. Only it wasn't in my handwriting. But it was on the same yellow-lined paper as the notes I useta write. An' I read it an' . . . and it saidÉit said, "Vanessa . . . I love you. Your Uncle Charlie." Thass what it said. "Vanessa, I love you. Your Uncle Charlie." I dunno where it is anymore. I dunno where I put it. I wish I'da took better care of it.

Information on this playwright may be found at www.smihandkraus.com. Click on the AUTHORS tab.

Row After Row

Jessica Dickey

Dramatic
Leah, late twenties to thirties

> *Leah just experienced the re-enactment of the infamous Pick-ett's Charge, considered the battle that was the turning point of the Civil War. She is speaking to two veteran re-enactors about her experience.*

> *Author's line breaks.*

LEAH: It was different than I expected.
    It was definitely interesting . . .
    I don't know . . . Stomping through the fields, the gear clanging against my thighs and back, making an ugly bell sound, my pack against my shoulder . . . All the motion of gear on the body, all these physical sensations were just immediately interesting to me, like I couldn't stop feeling my body or something, which actually I haven't been able to do in a long time . . . And my legs—my left and my right, climbing, the swish of grass, my left and my right, gliding next to and then past each other . . . And even though it's fake, you know—you know it's fake—I still felt scared and excited, a kind of sweaty anticipation.
    The sun was high, and there were hundreds of us climbing across this field, toward the trees on the other side . . . And suddenly—there they were—the *other* thousands, wearing the *other* color, but the same gear, the same pack, the same sweat. And that's the only clarity there was—the journey, the arriving, seeing them for the first time . . . And then the rest was chaos—we started through the field—and I found myself screaming at the top of my lungs, just hollering like a fucking lunatic! How often do you get to do that?! Just ROAR like a fucking WILD BOAR. And because you WANT to, not because you're in trouble and you have to or whatever . . . And yet I kept looking around like, what the

fuck are we doing? Why are we doing this? And I kind of loved that— the futility of it, you know? And somewhere near the end of the field I got hit and went down. Just like that.

And then I just lie there and listened. To my breath, to the other men charging around me, sometimes over me, my chest scratched and hot from the charge.

I listened to the earth, the sunshine.

There was a man who went down near me, and I could see his white hand in the sun, extra bright, like coral or a flag. The gentle curl of his fingers in the grass seemed to say, Touch me;

or—Let me rest;

or—Behold;

or— Soft high five. ☺

And then suddenly I wondered if the dead were watching— watching us— sitting in their invisible chairs, in their invisible rows, shaking their heads at these crazy assholes who actually want to relive this terrible moment.

And then I think I took a nap.

The whole thing was more fun—and more sad—than I was expecting.

But after going through it, I can see why people come back.

Keep trying—to catch—a *glimpse* . . .

RX

Kate Fodor

Comic
Allison, thirties to forties

Allison is the Marketing Director for a large pharmaceuticals company, here revealing at a shareholders' meeting that the company has a new drug in development which will alleviate workplace depression.

ALLISON: Wow, great presentation. Thanks, Carl. It's always good to hear about what's going on in the cardiology business unit. They've got a lot of heart over there. For those of you who haven't heard me speak at a shareholder's meeting before, I'm Allison Hardy, MBA, team leader of the Neurology Business Unit here at Schmidt Pharma. One of the things we are especially excited to share with you this year is a development-stage drug we've code-named SP-925, which targets workplace depression, a newly identified—and we believe eminently treatable—disease caused by a startling drop in norepinephrine levels during the working day. Plummeting norepinephrine levels leave some sufferers listless and unproductive, while others become agitated and difficult to work with. Anyone have a colleague they'd like to volunteer for our clinical trial? Put your hands down, I'm kidding! We're in the process of pre-screening subjects for the first major efficacy trial of SP-925, and we'll have that data to present to you at the next annual Schmidt Pharma shareholders meeting, assuming all goes well. And while I am required by the SEC to caution you that my presentation today has contained forward-looking statements that are not guarantees of future performance and involve a number of risks and uncertainties, I assure you that I intend to personally see to it that all goes well. Now ask me some questions so I can stay up here a little longer. I love it up here.

*Information on this playwright may be found at
www.smihandkraus.com. Click on the AUTHORS tab.*

Sex Curve

Merridith Allen

Comic
Robyn, twenty-seven to thirty-two

Robyn, a sex lit writer and columnist, decides she needs to educate her two roommates about how to pick a potential boyfriend.

ROBYN: "The compatibility trifecta." There are three key factors which will help determine how a man will act. The first factor is porn. Yes, it may be uncomfortable for you, the potential love interest, to immediately dive into your potential mate's porn collection. However, his sexual habits, stamina and personality are all reflected through his porn. *(She looks over to LUCAS, who is chewing. She swats at him.)*
Lucas, are you chewing gum? Spit it out. Anyway, the second factor is friends. Get to know his friends, and you get to know the side of himself that you may not see or know or come across otherwise. Friends have all the right character revealing stories. Lastly, look at his habits. This is an extension of factor one, but includes both sexual and non sexual habits. Things such as masturbation frequency, diet, exercise, sleep cycle, work schedule, hobbies and past relationship patterns all fit into this category. After a thorough investigation, if the result is pleasing, then go ahead, hop into bed with the guy.

Information on this playwright may be found at www.smihandkraus.com. Click on the AUTHORS tab.

STICK FLY

Lydia R. Diamond

Dramatic
Cheryl, late teens, African American

Cheryl is spending her summer working as a housekeeper for a wealthy black family which owns a home on Martha's Vineyard. Here, near the end of the play, she confronts the family and, in particular, its pater familias, about the truth of who her father really is.

CHERYL: I know Dr. LeVay. I know everything. And how the hell didn't not one of you sorry mothafuckas not figure it out . . . because you don't think 'bout nothin' but yourselves and your damn socio-economic bantering, and bugs, and relationship dysfunction and shit. Seriously the most self-involved bullshit people. *(beat)*. Mrs. LeVay found out. She came home and told that man that she knew he was my Daddy. Then she kicked your ass out the house, didn't she Dr. LeVay. And he brings his sorry ass up here.

So you knew and you looked me in the face and said,—you know how I like my sandwiches, or some shit like that . . . So, Two weeks ago . . . One of Mrs. LeVay's friends invites her to sit on the board at the high school where I'm where I'm supposed to be on scholarship, right. It's a big ole' lunch in some sort of fancy oak paneled room . . . . This is how it got told to my mama anyway, you know there's a network of maids . . . they talk . . . So, The Ladies who Lunch are lunching, and this woman says, —Michelle, it's so generous what your husband has been doing for that girl all these years. Eighteen years . . . , you can keep your mouth shut for five more minutes . . . . Imagine it . . . you could smell the money, all those skinny rich bitches staring at her over their shrimp salads.—Four years now, right, Michelle? Mrs. LeVay's been set up. Your Daddy's been paying my tuition there since I started. Fought to have me accepted, but insisted it remain on the DL (to Kimber) that's down low. Twenty-Five-thousand a year. So, this is the thing that's the craziest. It wasn't that Mrs. LeVay was broken up about a kid who shares her own kids gene pool washing her crusty sheets, no, the tragedy was that it got out. She calls my mother, threatens to fire her . . . calls her all out of her name, after Ma's been so quiet about it all these years . . . and threatens to take us to court for libel. I'm supposed to have a daddy got shot in the gulf . . . And you knew . . . how can you live with yourself?

STICK FLY

Lydia R. Diamond

Dramatic
Taylor, twenty-seven, African American

> *Taylor is the daughter of renowned public intellectual James
> Bradley Scott. She was raised by a single mother college
> professor. Though she carries his name, and so has had
> entrée to some social privileges, her father was not a part of
> her life. She also has gone without financially. She is visit-
> ing her boyfriend and his family, who own a large home on
> Martha's Vineyard. Here, she is talking about racial attitude
> she encountered in college which infuriated her.*

TAYLOR: It's all relative. From where I sit the bulk of the
racial stuff they get is that people assume they're smart,
guys want to date them, and they fit all of the shoes on the
sales rack. And one of the Beckys says—like, what do you
mean, color distinctions? And I look at the professor, with
her pageboy-Birkenstock-unshaved ass and she's not giving
it up. So I'm on. And I explain that not only is it problematic
that we haven't stopped to consider racial tensions in our
now female dominated society, but we haven't even begun
to consider class. Fine. So one of the Becky's gets quite
hostile, and then just down right ignorant, and eventually
she was saying that if it was a Utopian society there would
be only one dominant race, and the teacher is agreeing and
I'm trying to show them that this would not be a Utopian
society, that this would be the Third Reich . . . and the Asian
girl is saying it's just for purposes of discussion, but she's
clearly very upset. But this is the kicker, I get a call from
the professor the next day. She'd like to apologize for let-
ting things get out of control. She's pretty sure that at some
point things may have become racist, and I say, I think it
started when you decided to teach a class called feminist
voices of the 20th century and include no women of color.
Well, she explains there really aren't women of color ac-

cepted in the canon of hard feminist discourse. And then she misquotes my Dad back to me as if he would support such nonsense. He would, but still, she doesn't know that. I guess it was the last straw or something. That was it. I'd been fighting pretty much the same battle since high school. I was tired. I was supposed to be getting an education, but instead, I'm teaching cultural sensitivity 101 every time I turn around, and have been since like, third grade. So I go home and take a shower and turn on my little laptop, and it's so pretty and I select Vegas style . . . and I play and sleep and occasionally eat and I don't stop playing.

The Submission

Jeff Talbott

Dramatic
Emilie, twenties to thirties. African American

> *Danny is a young gay playwright who wrote a play about an
> inner city black family under a pseudonym that appears to
> be a black woman, believing that nobody would do the play
> if they knew it was by a white guy. Miraculously, a major
> regional theatre accepts the play for production, and Danny
> has hired Emilie to be his "front." The plan was that Emilie
> would "out" herself opening night during a curtain speech
> Danny wrote for her—but she didn't. Here, she lays into
> Danny for his political and racial views.*

EMILIE: You know what I can't get over? You know what
amazes me? Because on a certain level, some place in me,
I get it, Danny. I get it. I get this mentality you have. I hear
you. Because all of that must be frustrating. Really. But
what stops me is that you can spout such bullshit within a
blink of saying how sympathetic you are, how we're the
same. It's such a fuckin' load that I wish . . . Maybe it's
the gay thing, right? Maybe it's the fact that you've either
spent so much time on your knees or facing the headboard
that you literally can't keep anything straight. Get it? Can't
keep anything straight? It's such bullshit that you can spend
your time, and maybe this is both of you, maybe it's all of
you, I don't know, I'm certainly not going to stoop to some
"you people" kind of statement, not like you did, I'm just
not built that way. But it's fucking ridiculous that you can
look at the world and identify all the places where you think
people are less than you because they can't understand your
whatever, your fucking pain, even if they've been through
some of the same waters. And not just because those theatres
you're so mad at, those places that, whatever you said, just
give away some percentage of their season to, you know,
to . . . us. Yeah, us. Well, they are all run by fucking gay

men. All of them. Fucking most of them. Gay men taking away your, Jesus, your precious birthright and handing it over to all those awful, talent-free black folk. Makes your whole point seem a little . . . what's the word? Gay. And you're right, I don't know what high school was like for you, I don't know what it was like to be last on the bench for dodge ball or whatever. What it was like, what it must've been like to not be able to choose between Maria and Anita for who you'd most like to be in fuckin' *West Side Story*. Oh, no, I know, that's not what you said. You're much more worried about how awful it was that some Equal Opportunity history teacher spent a few too many days on how hard life was on a plantation for your sweet little palate. That must have really, really sucked. I get it. But the time for me to sit still and take your bullshit pie like dessert is done now. So, I'm sorry I took your fuckin' play away from you, but I'm starting to think it wasn't yours to begin with. You may have written it, but given your dirty little mouth, I probably saved you a ton of embarrassment by talking tonight. Because you would've stuck your fat foot in that dirty hole and the thing would be back in a drawer. You should thank me, Danny. Because my guess is this fuckin' play is all you got. And the big sick irony is, in the end, you may have written one good thing, but you still needed a black woman to get anybody to pay attention.

Information on this playwright may be found at
www.smithandkraus.com. Click on the AUTHORS tab.

SUNLIGHT

Sharr White

Dramatic
Charlotte, late thirties

> *Years ago, Charlotte Gibbon narrowly escaped the World*
> *Trade Center attacks. Ever since, her plight has been a*
> *subject of an epic struggle between her father, a liberal lion*
> *and president of a private Northeastern university, and her*
> *husband, a conservative dean of the law school. Her father*
> *and husband have just physically fought with one another.*

CHARLOTTE: STOP IT! BOTH OF YOU! STOP IT! Get off!
You get off of him Vince, now, get off! Now get up, look
at you, you're like a couple of children! I mean every day
there's a new thumb in the eye! And for what! Yes, Vince?
Still want to bring my mail to Greece? Be my guest, the
two of you can wake up and have a nice breakfast then go
slit each other's throats in the Aegean sea. Or better yet you
can do battle at the temple on the hill because who cares
what you destroy, everything's already in ruins.
(To Vincent.)
Don't you see? What I mean when I say I. Don't. Know? I
mean look at us. I don't know how we're all going to make
it. That man right there, I don't know how he's going to
survive in the wild. He thinks ice magically appears in the
bucket and that when he shouts, dinner just appears on the
table. And you, so help you God, you're going to save me
even if it kills me. I don't know why you're so concerned
with averting the end of the world, Vince, when everybody
knows the end of the world . . . it already happened. And
me, I know how to live . . . more. I know how to live . . .
longer. But I, I, don't know. How to live . . . again. How will
I live again . . . How will I live again? Daddy I think I've
just changed my mind, I'm not going with you to Greece.
And I can't stay here to help you out of this mess, Vince.
I think I should go . . . somewhere else. For a while. And

maybe if the dust has settled when I get back and somebody can figure out how we can all make it, then, perhaps . . . I don't know.

Information on this playwright may be found at www.smithandkraus.com. Click on the AUTHORS tab.

The Tutor

Kate Mulley

Comic
Meredith, late twenties

Meredith, a Yale Law School graduate turned SAT tutor, is recording a video diary entry for her used underwear website.

MEREDITH: I know what you're thinking: How does a nice smart girl get involved in petty sex trade? Two parts necessity, one part childhood repression. But seriously: I read an article about it. It's 3L spring and despite having some pretty impressive credentials and a desire to change the world, I can't find a job. My father, who's a *philosopher*, tells me I should think outside the box for once and focus on the present rather than the future. So I spend a lot of time perusing the internet in hopes that it would pique my imagination. One week I decided I would join the Peace Corps, until I realized that I didn't really want to live in any of the countries they go to. After that I thought I would open up a cupcake store, but student loans and a lack of decorating skills made that plan pretty ludicrous. Not to mention it's an utter cliché at this point. And then I read an article about used underwear retail. And the more research I did, the more intrigued I was. When you feel like you were the least sexually active girl at a school like Brown, sometimes you need to prove your past wrong by living in the present. So, I enlisted a photographer friend to help me with pictures, used my nerdy high school computer skills to build a kickass site and went live a month later. It started out slow, but an ingenious viral campaign and some innuendo-laden tweeting made my site the one to watch pretty quickly. By the time graduation rolled around I was making bank and was too busy to study for the bar, which I determined was unnecessary anyway. That fall, I started SAT tutoring to give myself a slightly more legitimate supplement to my sexy online business. And voila. A year later, I'm financially solvent, in constant contact with 75 perverted men and 5 women and the lingerie store down the street calls me when any new items come in stock. And you wonder why I haven't had sex in a month?

Information on this playwright may be found at
www.smithandkraus.com. Click on the AUTHORS tab.

When January Feels Like Summer

Cori Thomas

Dramatic
Nirmala, forties, East Indian

Nirmala is speaking to her husband Prasad who is in an irreversible coma. He is hooked up to machines which are keeping him alive.

NIRMALA: I've told Ishan that I hate you but I don't hate you. If you hear me Prasad, I don't hate you. But I hate what you have done to me. You took a young girl from India. And you promised her parents you would be a good husband, but you weren't. How you made me feel. A handsome man like you. And everyone thought you wanted me to be your wife because you thought I was beautiful and suitable. Because my family was low compared to yours, how could I say something. What would my mother think of the real reason I have no children? The doctor says you're not improving. But I can't kill you. I've thought about why I sit here waiting. I'm waiting to understand why I wear a red bindi and call you my husband, and work at your shop, and cook and clean even though you never . . . On our wedding night, I waited for you. I heard you snore and I knew you were asleep. And I thought it was the days of fun and dancing. And we left India the next day, so then I thought it was the time difference, that perhaps you were tired from the traveling. Every night, I waited for you to turn towards me and enjoy me but you never did. And when I used to look at you, I thought . . . I'm lucky. My eyes were very pleased by what I saw, Prasad. And I could imagine you touching my cheek, or touching my arms, or my legs, and my back, and my neck, and my skin. And I wished you would. Every minute I wished you would, even just once. One night I turned to your back and I put my arm around you and I felt your body pull away from me, and I felt you hold your breath, and I could almost hear you saying "don't, don't, don't . . . touch me" And so I turned back to my own side. I took my arm from around you and I turned away to my own side.

(beat)

After they shot you, I put those magazines in a box and closed it with tape. And I wrote the word trash on it. I put away your days and days and weeks and nights and months and minutes of magazines with unclothed women who don't look like me at all. Those aren't even real people that you know, Prasad. I'm sure you never knew those people. But you preferred them to me. And now people have seen that box. Ishan has seen it. Joe has seen it, I know he has. And now they know you did not find me pleasing. How can you still be hurting me from there? Well, now, these days, if I want, I can lift your arm and put your hand close to my skin, and make you touch me. And you can't move away. Here is my chance at last to feel your skin next to mine. But it's not the same is it? What good will it do?

(beat)

But I can't let these people unplug this machine. Even though I have a good reason, I can't do it. Every morning I wake and I wash my face, and I brush my teeth, and I comb my hair, and I place the bindi to my forehead and I remember what it means to wear one. It means that I'm your wife, Prasad, whether or not you liked it. It means that I'm your wife until you die.

Information on this playwright may be found at www.smithandkraus.com. Click on the AUTHORS tab.

SCENES

3 To A Session: A Monster's Tale

Desi Moreno-Penson

Seriocomic
Ally and Paula, mid- to late twenties to late thirties

Ally and Paula are playing roles in this scene. The scene appears to be something out of a cheesy 'adult' video. Ally is 'playing the role' of being a mentally disturbed individual who just can't seem to stop flirting with her 'therapist' Paula. In this scene, Paula is obviously having trouble keeping in character mainly because she is becoming increasingly flustered (as well as aroused) by Ally's sexual advances. However, as Ally's 'seduction' of Paula continues, it becomes evident that her real self threatens to rise to the surface.

PAULA: Which one is yours?

ALLY: They're all mine. All of them.

PAULA: *(holding up a thong)* Even this?

ALLY: *(smiling)* Especially that one.

PAULA: *(Folds up the thong; tosses it back in the box.)* How can anyone wear something that feels so restrictive . . . so tight . . . Right up your . . .
(embarrassed) . . . You know?

ALLY: Up my ass.

PAULA: Yeah. There.

ALLY: Why don't you find out? Put them on.

PAULA: Um . . .

ALLY: How do you think that would make you feel?

PAULA: *(out of character)* No . . . you don't ask that . . . I ask that . . . *(back in character)* How does wearing thong panties make you feel?

ALLY: Sexy.

PAULA: Do you like to feel sexy?
(Ally reaches out for the small, plastic sprayer on a table next to her.)

ALLY: Water is sexy.

PAULA: Is it?

ALLY: *(fondling the small spray can)* Oh yeah…steam rising up from the tub, warming your skin . . . the door locked . . . next to the toilet, I found a copy of—

PAULA: *Hustler.*

ALLY: *(pointing the sprayer at her)* No. Screw. *Penthouse.*

PAULA: What are you doing?

ALLY: I'm going to spray you.

PAULA: Why?

ALLY: Because I want to see you wet.

PAULA: Okay, let's back-pedal a little bit here. I sense you feel threatened.

ALLY: Are you threatening me?

PAULA: Maybe you think I am. You feel you need to do something to me. You want to get me wet. So, I'll feel small . . . embarrassed . . . helpless. You want to humiliate me.
(a beat) If it makes you feel better—

ALLY: Yes?

PAULA: Then you can spray me.

ALLY: (eager) Oh, *goody* . . .

PAULA: But—*(Ally's hand freezes.)*

ALLY: What?

PAULA: Not in the face, okay?
(Ally pauses, frustrated. She sprays PAULA in the knee area. PAULA cries out in arousal.)

PAULA: *(composing herself)* So, Ally—how did that make you feel?

ALLY: Not as good as I would've liked. But that's okay. I like playing doctor with you.

PAULA: Please don't say things like that.

ALLY: Except now I think I'd like to have a *physical* . . . !

PAULA: As your therapist, I'm not going to be able to treat you properly if you continue to distract me.

ALLY: Yes, I understand that, but—I'm the distracting one, right? I mean I'm the nut here, right?

PAULA: Please don't refer to yourself that way.

ALLY: Do you know why I'm here?

PAULA: Yes. You claim to see visions.

ALLY: *(amorous; checking out her legs)* Yes . . . yes, I see *visions* . . .!

PAULA: Do you want to tell me a little bit about some of these visions?

ALLY: I never remember any. They come and go. If you give me a name, I might be able to remember *something* but other than that . . .

(Shrugs her shoulders.)

PAULA: Yes. They overtake you in the moment. Like memory.

ALLY: Yes. They come and go.

PAULA: Yes. Like memory.

ALLY: Yes.

(a beat)

Open your legs for me.

PAULA: What did you say?

ALLY: Let me see it—

PAULA: See what?

ALLY: The monster.

PAULA: Ally—

ALLY: No? You won't show me your little monster?

PAULA: I'm not here for your amusement—don't play games.

ALLY: But you like my games.

PAULA: No one likes your games. This is serious. You've been placed here because you claim to be channeling the spirit of *Moisefina*, a converted, Sephardic nun from 15th century Spain.

ALLY: Holy shit.

PAULA: *(looking through a folder)* And according to your file, before she became a nun, this *Moisefina* was some kind of a *button-weaver* and she felt the Spaniards were stealing all of her father's buttons. So, she wanted *you* to bring her as many buttons as you could. In fact, she wanted *all* the buttons in the world. And in your zeal, you tackled about three people to the ground and one of them, a local priest, sustained major nose injuries. *You almost broke his nose!*

ALLY: Well, he should've given me the fucking button then, right?

(Ally dissolves into laughter.)

PAULA: *(gives her a withering look.)* If you can't take this seriously—

ALLY: *(teasingly)* Aww . . . don't be mad . . . I only hurt you because I love you . . .

PAULA: You love me because you hurt me.

ALLY: What?

PAULA: You hurt me because you love me.

ALLY: *(out of character)* Wait a minute . . . why are you saying that? That's not what you're supposed to say . . .

PAULA: *(out of character as well)* What am I supposed to say?

ALLY: *(still out of character)* What do you mean? You know . . . *you know* . . . about how I need discipline…this is the part where we talk about how I need to be *disciplined* by the hospital orderly—

PAULA: Oh. *Oh!* (Back in character) You're so undisciplined—

ALLY: Yes, yes, I am.

PAULA: You're thinking about him again, aren't you? The handsome, muscular orderly who's standing right outside this office? The one who's like He-Man?

ALLY: *(defiantly)* Maybe.

PAULA: You're thinking about him, aren't you? About what might happen if he came in here?

ALLY: Maybe I am . . . so what is it to you?

PAULA: You think about his wild eyes. His bulging arms and powerful chest. The hair on his legs.

ALLY: You think about him, too.

PAULA: Yes, yes you're right. I do. The one who's like He-Man?

ALLY: Yes. He-Man.

PAULA: I'm so undisciplined. Just like you. I'm a dirty girl.

ALLY: *(echoes this.)* I'm a dirty girl.

PAULA: If it was just the three of us in here, in this office . . . all alone . . . just the three of us . . . quiet . . . with the door locked—

ALLY: Maybe you should call him in.

PAULA: Now? Right now?

ALLY: Yeah. Right now. I think perhaps I *do* need discipline from the handsome, muscular hospital orderly . . . with the hairy legs . . . and the only way I'm going to get what I deserve is by having him come in and *give it to me*. Now. Where is he?

PAULA: *(pointing towards the pitcher of juice)* He's right behind that door. He's sooo close.

ALLY: My mouth is dry.

PAULA: Are you thirsty? Thirsty for He-Man's kisses?

ALLY: Yes. Yes, I'm thirsty.

PAULA: Then have some orange juice.

Information on this playwright may be found at www.smihandkraus.com. Click on the AUTHORS tab.

. . . AND LA IS BURNING

Y. York

Seriocomic
Sylvia, forty-seven
Haddie, forty-five

> *. . . AND LA IS BURNING is a comedy set against the back-
> drop of the 1992 national tragedy following the acquittal of
> the four police officers accused of beating up Rodney King.
> What happens when two middle-aged White women and a
> younger African-American man try to negotiate the intersect-
> ing terrains of well-intentioned liberalism, racism, the work-
> place, the news, reality, and the Cosby Show. In this scene
> Sylvia, a visiting Harvard scholar, interrogates her neighbor
> Haddie, a low-level federal employee, over coffee.*

HADDIE: He's always whining about how he's black, how he's
    can't get anything because he's black. Let him try being a
    woman, see how far he gets being a woman. Soon as you're
    a woman you don't get any breaks. Not from the guy bosses
    not from the women bosses, the women bosses, they're worse.
    They want to keep you down to make out like they're really
    special because they got a supervisor job and you just didn't
    try hard enough, just didn't stay in school long enough.
SYLVIA: They say this to you?
HADDIE: I know what they're thinking. And notice how they're
    all pretty? Makes you wonder how they got their jobs.
SYLVIA: The female supervisors—?
HADDIE: Pretty, flirting, smart mouths on them, too. "Witty." My.
    Aren't they witty. I don't think she's witty. I don't know what
    they're laughing at half the time, and I don't care—tells me
    to recycle and then when I do leaves me anonymous notes.
SYLVIA: Who are you talking about—?
HADDIE: Let them laugh—she can't fire me—Ha! This is the
    government, and they can't fire you, and there's no cause to
    fire me because I work hard and sometimes more than eight
    hours.

SYLVIA: When you say "they" do you mean your female supervisor?

HADDIE: What?

SYLVIA: You're saying "they" and "she" and I wonder if these pronouns have the same antecedent noun. *(brief pause)* It's a pronoun-antecedent . . . thing.

HADDIE: *(teaching)* When I say *they* it's *they,* and when I say *she* it's *she.*

SYLVIA: Uh huh. And you think your supervisor slept her way into her job?

HADDIE: How could I know *that?*

SYLVIA: But you said—never mind . . . Do you get overtime?

HADDIE: It's the federal government. You don't get squat.

SYLVIA: I thought government jobs were the good ones. Like you said, it's hard to get fired. And you know as long as there is a government you'll get your paycheck.

HADDIE: (Panic.) What do you mean, as long as there's a government? Where is the government going?

SYLVIA: Nowhere. That's the point.

HADDIE: Then you shouldn't say it's going away.

SYLVIA: I'm interested in something you said . . . about how people use the term "racist" as they once indicted with the word "communist." (brief pause.) Did your unit partner call you a racist?

HADDIE: *(horror)* Are you writing stuff down?

SYLVIA: Do you mind?

HADDIE: I thought you just wanted to be friends.

SYLVIA: *(caught)* I'm a writer. We write things down. It's the dangerous thing about knowing a writer. We write things down.

HADDIE: In shorthand?

SYLVIA: Sometimes in shorthand.

HADDIE: Do you write novels?

SYLVIA: You don't know what I write?

HADDIE: No. The handyman said you're the writer. That's all I know.

SYLVIA: I write about economic disparity . . .
(clarifying)
Economic inequality. History. Basically nonfiction. Like that.

HADDIE: I like novels.

SYLVIA: . . . What kind?

HADDIE: Short ones. So they're not so heavy at night. In bed.

SYLVIA: A standard criterion.

HADDIE: I dropped a book on my nose once. I was holding it like this and I fell asleep. Dropped it right on my nose.

SYLVIA: Must have hurt.

HADDIE: No, it was short. I think writers are interesting.

SYLVIA: That's because writers make writers the most interesting characters in their novels. *(Sylvia laughs, Haddie doesn't.)* Just a little joke—in my experience, they're not that interesting. What does he say, your black colleague, when he complains?

HADDIE: *(surprised)* He doesn't complain.

SYLVIA: I thought . . . You said he complains that it's unfair, that promotions are unfair.

HADDIE: He *thinks* it . . . he doesn't say it. He thinks it. He'll say it, though. Once he's been in the office a little longer. He'll say it.

SYLVIA: I see. Did he grow up in Seattle?

HADDIE: I don't know.

SYLVIA: It's just that, some of the black neighborhoods, they're pretty bad.

HADDIE: Dangerous.

SYLVIA: No, not dangerous, well, maybe. But rundown. Demoralized. High Point? It would be hard to make it on your own, coming out of a neighborhood like High Point.

HADDIE: I didn't have it easy.

SYLVIA: Have you been there?

HADDIE: No, but I know. You just have to pull yourself up.

SYLVIA: By the bootstraps?

HADDIE: Bootstraps. That's what I think, too.

SYLVIA: No, I don't—

(sighs)

There are some tough neighborhoods, that's all I'm saying.

HADDIE: I don't know where he grew up . . . What kind of novel are you writing?

SYLVIA: It's not . . . it's a non-fiction . . . novel.

HADDIE: What's it about?

SYLVIA: Pernicious systems—*hidden* systems. Race. America.

HADDIE: . . . You ever notice how people don't listen?

SYLVIA: Oh, yes.

HADDIE: You listen. I think that's interesting.

(After the briefest of pauses, Sylvia puts away her notebook and stands to go.)

SYLVIA: Well, goodness, thanks a lot. I have to go. I have things I need to prepare for work tomorrow.

HADDIE: You want to get coffee again tomorrow night?

SYLVIA: I'm busy tomorrow night. I think I have to work late. All week in fact.

HADDIE: Okay. I'll watch TV or something.

SYLVIA: Great.

HADDIE: I like to keep up with the trial. The L.A. cops trial.

(brief pause)

SYLVIA: You're following the trial?

HADDIE: Yes, from the beginning. I'm fascinated.

SYLVIA: I'M . . . interested in it myself.

HADDIE: It's fascinating.

SYLVIA: You know, maybe we could get together after all.

HADDIE: You don't have to work late?

SYLVIA: I'll work late next week.

HADDIE: Okay. Same time, same station. Right here at the deli counter.

Information on this playwright may be found at www.smihandkraus.com. Click on the AUTHORS tab.

BECHNYA

Saviana Stanescu

Dramatic
Shari, early thirties
Vicky, late twenties

> *Bechnya is a play about the confrontation between two women
> who share a past and negotiate a future. It's another sad
> yet funny story about political and familial circumstances
> that determine people's lives; and ultimately Bechnya is an
> arresting glimpse into the complex world of international
> adoptions. Shari faces hopeless days and nights in Bechnya,
> a fictional country torn by wars and poverty. The American
> Dream takes unsettling forms in Shari's mind as she is a
> prisoner in a dark cell with only one escape: her imagination.
> So she imagines—or maybe recalls—a meeting with Fatma,
> a Bechnyan girl now living in America. Vicky plays Fatma
> in her imagination.*

    Lights up on Shari and Vicky in the living room.
SHARI: I am a bad girl, Fatma. I came here to kill you and set
    your house on fire.
VICKY: *(beat)* You don't have the heart to do this.
SHARI: I don't know about my heart.
    (She starts to take off her clothes.)
I'm bad. I'm a bad girl. My name is Shari. Shari. Shari is bad.
    Shari is a baaad girl.
VICKY: What are you doing, Shari?
SHARI: Stay still. I will let you go soon.
VICKY: Stop this, please, stop it!
SHARI: I am going to sit on white embers.
VICKY: Let me help you, Shari.
SHARI: You don't remember me . . . (p*ause)*
SHARI: It's OK . . . It's OK, Fatma. Why to remember, what's
    so good in remembering?
VICKY: Look. You can stay here with me. For however long
    you want.

SHARI: This is not my house.

VICKY: You can make it here in America. I can help you.

SHARI: It's too late.

VICKY: It's never too late.

SHARI: I love this American lie . . .

VICKY: You can be our . . . nanny! Emma will love you! Even
/ Michael will . . .

SHARI: I don't want to lie in front of children.

VICKY: There's no need to lie. You can be yourself, always
tell the truth.

SHARI: Then I would have to teach them Bechnyan. Talk with
them in Bechnyan.

VICKY: You speak very good English.

SHARI: I learned English only to speak to you.

VICKY: Then talk to me! Tell me about you. I want to know
everything about you.

SHARI: My little liar . . .

VICKY: What does Shari mean in Bechnyan?

SHARI: A silly thing. Love.

VICKY: But that's beautiful! To be called love. And Fatma?

SHARI: Destiny.(She continues stripping.)

VICKY: Please, put your clothes on, Shari. Please!

*(By now Shari is almost naked. She points the gun at
Vicky.)*

SHARI: Don't move!

*(She unties Vicky, then sits in the white chair with the gun
still pointing at Vicky.)*

VICKY: Shari. Love. Nothing is utterly bad and irreversible . . .
This is not a horror movie . . . Put your clothes on! I'm going
to cook a nice dinner for us . . . A five-star dinner!

SHARI: Come here and kneel d own!

VICKY: Shari . . .

(Shari shoots the teddy-bear.)

VICKY: No! Why are you doing this?

SHARI: Come here! . . . Come! . . .

VICKY: What do you wanna do? You don't have to do this.
Don't do this, Shari!

SHARI: *(pushing Vicky down)* Lick my legs! Lick my feet, lick
my toes! Lick them!

VICKY: Shari . . .

SHARI: Lick them! Lick my skin! Lick!

VICKY: You can't ask / me to . . .

SHARI: (pushing Vicky down) Lick my feet when I say, lick! You owe me this, Fatma. Wipe off my sins with your tongue! Make me clean, Fatma. I want to be clean. When God sees me and asks me for my name, I want to answer: Snow-White. I am Snow-White . . . (Vicky starts licking Shari's calves. Shari lifts the hand with the gun and looks at it. She touches her own body with the gun.)Yeah . . . Lick my legs, tie them with your tongue, lick me, wipe me, bite me, little white rat-fairy...Yes . . . Don't stop! Bite! . . . Taste me. Chew me. Spit me up! Like a piece of rotten apple. Poisoned apple. Bite me, Fatma! Taste me. Remember me. Keep a piece of me with you, in you, Fatma . . . Don't leave me alone! . . . Leave me alone! . . . (Shari kisses the gun) Adala, Fatma . . . Adala.

VICKY: No! (beat) Kaneper! Kari! Zaka! Zaka! Zaka!

(Shari caresses Vicky with the gun. Shari smiles.)

SHARI: Zaka, Fatma, zaka. (She looks her in the eyes, raises the gun.)

Information on this playwright may be found at www.smihandkraus.com. Click on the AUTHORS tab.

Call Me Waldo

Rob Ackerman

Comic
Sarah, forties

> *Sarah is a nurse at a hospital on Long Island whose husband*
> *has suddenly started to channel the spirit of Ralph Waldo*
> *Emerson. Sarah confided in a doctor friend, Cynthia, also in*
> *her forties. Cynthia told Sarah not to panic, and Sarah took*
> *her advice, and even made love to her husband in his Emerson*
> *persona. Now Sarah awakens to the realization that she may*
> *find Emerson more attractive than her husband.*

SCENE 13: OFFICE

> *Sarah barges in on Cynthia.*

SARAH: Cynthia, you bitch.

CYNTHIA: Excuse me?

SARAH: You just wrecked my life.

CYNTHIA: What?

SARAH: Maybe I didn't totally love my husband, but I didn't have to HATE my husband.

CYNTHIA: What are you talking about?

SARAH: I HATE him. Totally HATE HIM. He makes me wanna HURL.

CYNTHIA: Why?

SARAH: I can't even tell you. I swear, unless you want me to BLOW CHUNKS on your shoes. I mean, I just slept with this man, this strong, confident man, this man who played me like a cello, and then I woke up with Mister Milquetoast.

CYNTHIA: Okay, now, that is not my fault.

SARAH: Yes it is. It's totally your fault. I drank the Kool Aid, but you mixed the Kool Aid. You stirred the poison with a spoon. I trusted you, I did what you said, and now what I say is: SCREW YOU, CYNTHIA!

CYNTHIA: Whoa, hold on. I just told you to listen.

SARAH: Well, I LISTENED!

CYNTHIA: You look flushed. What have you been up to? Where have you been?

SARAH: I've been readin'. I spent the whole bleepin' day in the bleepin' library.

CYNTHIA: I thought you were bleeping Waldo.

SARAH: After. I went after. You shoulda heard him when he woke up.

CYNTHIA: What'd he say?

SARAH: Oh man, he was such a wimp, such a total wuss, such a whiner.

CYNTHIA: And so you went to the library?

SARAH: 'Cause you told me to start readin', and I couldn't find the *Collected Works,* and I—

CYNTHIA: You read Emerson.

SARAH: And now I'm ruined, wrecked, forever—and I'm never gonna be the same again.

CYNTHIA: And that's a bad thing?

SARAH: Yeah, it is. It is, Cynthia. And, by the way, Emerson is NOT a REPUBLICAN!

CYNTHIA: Slow down, now.

SARAH: I'm not gonna slow down, so you better speed up, sister. Have you read *An Address*?

CYNTHIA: Uh . . .

SARAH: Emerson's Address to the Harvard Divinity School, Cambridge, 1838.

CYNTHIA: No, as a matter of fact, I haven't.

SARAH: Just a year after he talked about *The American Scholar*, Emerson goes back to Harvard, and he's on fire! He tells these preachers and wannabes that their churches stink, their sermons are worthless, and he'd rather sit in silence and watch the snow fall than listen to some old gas bag fill people full o' fear and shame, because Jesus was NOT sayin' he was the ONLY son of God, he was SETTIN' AN EX-AMPLE, tellin' us WE are God's kids JUST LIKE HIM!

CYNTHIA: That's called blasphemy. Sweetie. They used to burn you at the stake for that.

SARAH: You know what they did? They kicked him out. For thirty years. For thirty years Emerson was banned from the hollow halls of Harvard.

CYNTHIA: *"Hallowed."*

SARAH: I'm tellin' you—

CYNTHIA: — *"The Hallowed Halls"*—

SARAH: The man is a monster, a freakin' monster.

CYNTHIA: You really have been reading.

SARAH: Heck yeah, I've been readin'.

CYNTHIA: Look at you.

SARAH: Yeah. Look at me. I'm a wreck.

CYNTHIA: Why are you saying that?

SARAH: 'Cause it's true.

CYNTHIA: Well, I don't think I've ever seen you look more alive, Sarah.

SARAH: What good's it gonna do me?

CYNTHIA: I don't know.

SARAH: Oh. You don't know. She doesn't know.

CYNTHIA: You're angry.

SARAH: Yeah, I'm angry. My husband goes crazy and you tell me to just let it happen and I do and he's a stallion, and then he turns into a sissy and now I'm stuck! I'm just stuck! In the mud!

CYNTHIA: So what are you gonna do?

Information on this playwright may be found at www.smihandkraus.com. Click on the AUTHORS tab.

Cut

Crystal Skillman

Comic
Colette, twenty-six
Rene, thirty-one

> *In Cut three reality TV show writers (Danno, Colette and Rene) are forced to re-cut the season finale to their House-wives rip-off "The Ladies of Malibu" in three hours which forces them to confront the real truth of how their destructive actions over the past six weeks have affected each other. In the play, this scene is a flashback where we see a time how Colette and Rene began to really become friends.*

> *(Three weeks ago. Colette and Rene cramped against a wall in the bar of a fancy restaurant.)*

COLETTE: Are you okay? You don't look ok. I'm sorry it's taking so long. Fuck! Right, fuck! Bobby he'll get us a table—I'm just glad you came.

RENE: You have three seconds.

> *(Rene starts to go.)*

COLETTE: Okay. Shit. Shit I mean—

RENE: Done.

COLETTE: I'm sorry. I never meant to get you in trouble–thank you. My mom thinks that means: dinner, fancy restaurant. Of course for her that means Pina Coladas at BBQ's —*(RENE: tries to go)* Please. Please. Please. Please. Don't—

RENE: Why do you take that Jessica shit home with you?

COLETTE: I don't. I don't know. I didn't know they would search our bags. I can't believe you said it was yours. I can't believe they believed you.

RENE: Why?

COLETTE: We know you never make a mistake. You're so good at this reality shit. When I came out here to open a dance studio. OH MY GOD THAT SOUNDS LIKE THE DUMBEST THING EVER. But you—you have something you can do, I don't even know how you—

RENE: Oh give me a break.

COLETTE: You think I'm stupid, I get it.

RENE: You know Jaws.

COLETTE: Some shark eats naked ladies. What does that have to do with . . . ?

RENE: Story planning? It's Jaws. Perfect beginning, middle and end.

COLETTE: I don't . . .

RENE: Pick anybody.

COLETTE: Ohhhh . . . Danno.

RENE: Good one. Small Town is like 451 Studios. One guy Danno. Biggest fear: not being accepted, like being scared of the water. Shark is in the water.

COLETTE: This time it's personal.

RENE: Right. So he has to face his fear—go in the water. But scene by scene we discover what he wants.

COLETTE: To blow the fucking shark up!

RENE: To blow the fucking shark up.

COLETTE: Oh but like what's the shark for Danno?

RENE: See? Now that's. That's philosophy.

COLETTE: It's family.

RENE: What do you mean?

COLETTE: He's always googling flights home but never goes out. His sister, plays her tracks from her orchestra—no shit—that he put into his itunes but he never calls her.

RENE: So—pick scenes to show that conflict.

COLETTE: Like trying to do yoga on his lunch break in his office while burning incense, but coming out more stressed than ever.

RENE: "I believe!' I believe! I believe!" That's good, that's—
(Colette, continuing the "Jaws" storyboarding game:)

COLETTE: Oh and for you it's your kid right? That's what you care about. And your husband—I see him all the time in that Mercedes commercial.

RENE: He wants to do more than that. Just went to London. Acting Fellowship, he'll be back soon.

COLETTE: You must miss him.

RENE: I really do have to go okay? Tell Bobby thanks for—

COLETTE: Why did you do it? Stick up for me?

RENE: We've got three more weeks together. I don't want to start over with someone new.

COLETTE: Noooo. You like me.

RENE: Just—

COLETTE: What?

RENE: Just stop taking that shit home to watch and you'll be fine, ok?

COLETTE: Rene? If it ever does really go bad, and they're gonna . . . you'll let me know right.

I don't want to be one of those people taken down the hall, into a room. Get your coat. Get an email kind of thing. I want to go in my own way. Like . . . have respect you know. Does that make sense?

(beat)

RENE: How about, I'll wave.

COLETTE: So it's like I'm going on a trip! Something nice.

RENE: Yeah. Like that.

COLETTE: Danno—I know this is weird. Something about the way he says your name.

RENE: You are . . . I do.

COLETTE: What?

RENE: Like you. Colette.

COLETTE: Oh shit! Look Bobby got us a table!! Yay!

Dark Part Of The Forest

Tammy Ryan

Seriocomic
Joan and Karen, late thirties

> *Joan is having trouble adjusting to living out in the country. She is married to Bill, an Air Traffic Controller at the Pittsburgh airport who has grown increasingly distant since their move. Their twelve year old daughter Emily is also unhappy and giving Joan trouble. In this scene, Joan confides in her best friend Karen the reasons why she wanted to quit her job and move to the country in the first place.*

JOAN: Be glad you're single, that's all I can say.

KAREN: Sometimes I am, listening to all my married friends and their problems. Not that you two are having problems.

JOAN: I don't know what we're having. We haven't had sex in about a hundred years.

KAREN: Well, there you go.

JOAN: He's been working a lot of evenings.

KAREN: Wait up one night, a little vino, a little nightgown.

JOAN: *(considers for a beat, then shifting gears)* I HATE MOVING! I feel like my whole life is teetering on the edge of a huge canyon, when really everything's great. We've got this great house, which took a year to be built and I couldn't wait and now it's done and now we're here and I don't know what the hell I'm going to do out in the country.

KAREN: It's a long way from Queens.

JOAN: I want a sidewalk! So I can walk somewhere and get a cup of coffee.

KAREN: Maybe we can scrounge up a teabag. *(begins looking in a box)* How's Emily like it out here?

JOAN: She hates it, of course, there's nothing to do, a new school, she's having trouble making friends. Just one more reason to hate her mother. She should be home soon.

KAREN: Well, I miss you already.

JOAN: I didn't expect to feel so isolated. Tell me it's still a day trip. I can meet you for lunch next time.

KAREN: You better.

JOAN: We just thought, the city schools, Emily at this age. The drugs, the everything, I wanted to save her from all that.

KAREN: Drugs are all over.

JOAN: Guns? Gangs? They're not out here.

KAREN: Are you kidding? Every boy over five's got a gun out here.

JOAN: They're called—hunters.

KAREN: Yeah, and all you hear on the local news is the whacko stuff that happens. Some guy in Westmoreland County chops up his wife and stuffs her in a garbage can.

JOAN: I don't watch the news, and we're not in Westmoreland County.

KAREN: Doesn't matter, it's all depressed except for people like you building beautiful homes, meanwhile your neighbor's a sheep farmer.

JOAN: He is not.

KAREN: I saw some kind of farm animal.

JOAN: It's a goat, or something, it's the kid's pet.

KAREN: Whatever. It was eating grass.

JOAN: Are you trying to make me feel better, Karen?

KAREN: Look, not to make you worried, it's beautiful, really, but driving up that road to your house, reminded me of *Unsolved Mysteries*.

JOAN: Great.

KAREN: There's something to be said for the city. All those people around, keeping an eye on each other.

JOAN: I'm from New York, remember.

KAREN: Hey, Pittsburgh's a city, even if it's a baby city.

JOAN: Just say,—I told you so, and get it over with.

(SOUND of a not too distant gunshot)

KAREN: What the hell was that?

JOAN: I don't know. A hunter?

(beat)

What am I gonna do out here?

KAREN: *(referring to a plate of cookies)* Did you bake these?

(Joan nods, Karen bites into one.)

You know what you should do. Buy a horse.

JOAN: Oh, right, we can't buy furniture.

KAREN: You gotta do something for yourself. Take riding lessons. Horses are great. I took lessons somewhere out here when I was a teenager.

JOAN: Actually, there is something I want to do. Don't laugh.

KAREN: What?

JOAN: I want . . . to write a book.

KAREN: I didn't know you were a writer.

JOAN: I wrote poetry in college. You're laughing! Hey, I majored in English literature.

KAREN: You wanna write, like a novel?

JOAN: For young adults. Well, for girls. I want to write something for Emily, to help her at this age, you know, keep her—power. And that was part of the deal, moving out here. I wouldn't have to work at the bank; I could stay home and try to write. But I haven't had time yet . . .

KAREN: I think that's great.

JOAN: You do?

KAREN: Yeah, definitely. Girls need real stories, not Cinderella-romantic-love is gonna save you crap. Give em stories that can help them do something. Number one, don't take typing. I wish somebody told me that. That way you'd never end up working as a secretary in a bank having an affair with your married boss. Of course, there are perks; I'm not washing his socks. His wife does that. Oops. Sorry. You were saying. You're writing a book.

JOAN: It's stupid. Everything I think of is stupid. I have twelve years of children's books in my head, all I can think of is Once upon a time . . .

KAREN: Forget the books. What were you doing at her age?

JOAN: Forget it, I don't want to give her any ideas.

KAREN: They'd be cautionary tales, right?

JOAN: I keep thinking about something, but it's too dark really.

KAREN: Dark I like.

JOAN: No, this is weird.

KAREN: Weird is great. Kids love weird.

JOAN: I want to write a contemporary Rumpelstilskin.

KAREN: Yeah.

JOAN: There's this young girl, eleven or twelve, and she's in trouble and has a problem or something . . .

KAREN: Right . . . .

JOAN: And this little dwarf . . .

KAREN: Little people. You don't call them dwarves any-more.

JOAN: This weird little guy crawls into her bedroom window and helps her to solve the problem, right, and so now she's indebted to him—

KAREN: He crawls into her bedroom window?

JOAN: Will you let me explain it? The point is she has to name him, right, like in the real story. As soon as she names him he loses his power and she gains hers.

KAREN: Because . . . she guesses his name?

JOAN: As soon as I say it out loud, it sounds stupid.

KAREN: Maybe it'll be different on the page. You know how when you tell somebody about a movie, it's not the same thing as seeing it?

JOAN: Just say what you mean: you hate it.

KAREN: What do I know about novel writing?

JOAN: About as much as I do which is nothing.
    (beat)
    I should just learn to knit! If I knew how to knit, I could make sweaters. Then, I could teach Emily to knit and she'd have a craft, so she could identify herself by what she could do.

KAREN: Knitting?

JOAN: And not what she looked like! You should see how she's starving herself. I can't stand it.

KAREN: Cause it reminds you of yourself.

JOAN: I don't know what to do with her.

KAREN: Write the book.

JOAN: It's stupid, I'm stupid.

KAREN: Even if it is dumb, it'll keep you outta trouble and away from the farm animals.

Information on this playwright may be found at www.smihandkraus.com. Click on the AUTHORS tab.

ELECTRA

Don Nigro

Seriocomic
Carolyn Ryan, forty-seven
Lexie, twenty-eight

Electra takes place in Armitage, a small town in East Ohio, in
1920. Carolyn is an intelligent but unhappy and increasingly
unstable woman who has been responsible for her husband's
death, her daughter Jenna's being blamed for it and put in a
mental institution, and most recently for encouraging her son
Thomas to commit suicide. Her daughter Lexie, the only per-
son who knew of Carolyn's guilt, had been trying to persuade
Thomas to kill Carolyn and Jenna's husband Nick, Carolyn's
lover, when Thomas, troubled and unhappy, had committed
suicide instead. This is the evening of Thomas' burial. Carolyn
sits on the porch alone, her brain racing with tormenting im-
ages from her life: the false name her murderer husband had
assumed and given their family, stolen from a dead man in a
box car, a doll her mad daughter Jenna left on the roof in the
rain, her husband's obsession with ancient Greek, Jenna's fear
that Captain Hook's crocodile lived under her bed, and Loopy
Rye, the village idiot, who she has learned is actually her il-
legitimate father. At the grave site, a drunken Nick, filled with
guilt, anger and self-hatred, has raped Lexie and left. Lexie
returns to the house to finally confront her mother.

CAROLYN: Fireflies. A necklace of dead flies. Mold on dead
trees glows in the dark. I drink plum brandy and polish my
glockenspiel. I've lost the skeleton key. Stole his name off
a dead man in a box car. Everybody here is clown people.
A doll left on the roof in the rain. Men eaten by rats. Old
furniture and mirrors in the attic. The last raven sitting on
the cow. Dead languages. Nightmares about being attacked
by flies. The crocodile under the bed. No. I'm fine. I'm absolutely fine. There's nothing wrong with me. It's everybody
else. Where have they all gone? So lonely, here at the end
of the world. I wish the village idiot would come and talk

to me. Are you out there, Loopy?

(A figure appears in the shadows.)

Who is that? Who's lurking out there now? I've got a gun.
Well, I don't actually have a gun, but I've got a knife. Well,
I don't have a knife on me, but there's several in the kitchen.
Loopy? Papa?

(Lexie appears, clothing torn, dirty.)

LEXIE: It's just me.

CAROLYN: Well, it's about time you got home. Where have
you been? Chicago? Did you stop at a barn dance? Your
brother is dead and you leave your poor old mother home
alone to drink plum brandy and talk to the village idiot.

(Getting a better look at Lexie.)

What happened to you? You look like you were trampled
by gypsies.

LEXIE: Something in the cemetery.

CAROLYN: What is it? What's wrong? Where's Nick?

LEXIE: Nick's gone.

CAROLYN: What do you mean he's gone? Gone where?

LEXIE: He's gone. He's not coming back.

CAROLYN: He hasn't gone anywhere.

LEXIE: I'm pretty sure he stopped at the bank on the way out
of town, to pick up a basket of other people's cash.

CAROLYN: What's happened to you? Why are you such a
mess?

LEXIE: I'm sorry I don't look my best at the moment, Mother,
but my sister's husband, your lover, just happened to rape
me in the cemetery after we buried my brother.

CAROLYN: No he didn't. Nick wouldn't do a thing like that.

LEXIE: He raped my sister on their wedding night.

CAROLYN: He didn't rape anybody.

LEXIE: You he didn't need to rape. You probably raped him.

CAROLYN: Stop saying that horrible word. I don't understand.
Where's he gone?

LEXIE: Hopped a freight to nowhere. Someplace in Greece,
maybe. Everybody ends up in Greece, in the end. Greece
is where everything begins and ends.

CAROLYN: He's really gone? He didn't even say goodbye?

LEXIE: I tell my mother a man has just raped me, and she's
offended that he didn't stop and say goodbye to her.

CAROLYN: I don't believe any man has ever done anything to you that you didn't want him to. I know what kind of person you are. You've driven him away on purpose. My husband is dead and my son is dead and my daughter's in a madhouse and now you've driven away my only friend.

LEXIE: Friend? You call him your friend?

CAROLYN: He's gone and it's all your fault. Everything is your fault.

LEXIE: My fault? Everything is my fault?

CAROLYN: You've spent your whole life blaming me for everything. It's not my fault no man will have you. It's not my fault you haven't got the guts to stop sponging off your mother and get out on your own. It's not my fault that your poisonous hallucinations have driven your sister insane and your brother to suicide. And it's certainly not my fault that Nick preferred me to you. Sometimes men are driven mad by my beauty. I can't help that.

LEXIE: *(A roar of frustration and fury coming out as she rushes at Carolyn.)*

AHHHHHHHHHHHHHH.

(Lexie jumps on Carolyn, knocks her over, and begins hitting her.)

CAROLYN: Stop it. Stop that. Lexie. You're insane. I don't want to hurt you.

LEXIE: Well, I want to hurt you, you psychopath. It's not my fault. I'm just driven mad by your beauty.

(Straddling Carolyn on the ground, Lexie begins strangling her.)

CAROLYN: No. Stop. No. Lexie.

(Carolyn manages to get her own hands around Lexie's throat and now the two of them are strangling each other, rolling back and forth.)

LEXIE: Monster. Monster. Monster.

CAROLYN: Ingrate. Ingrate.

(Carolyn hits Lexie in the face, stunning her, and then begins strangling her. Lexie's arms are down. Then Carolyn stops. She takes her hands from Lexie's neck, gets off her, and sits on the ground beside her.)

LEXIE: *(Coughing and gagging.)* What's the matter? Why did you stop?

CAROLYN: Because you're my daughter.

LEXIE: Because I'm your daughter? What kind of a reason is that? You have a chance to kill me and now finally I'm your daughter?

CAROLYN: You're just like me, you know.

LEXIE: Like you? I'm like you?

CAROLYN: You're the most like me of any of my children.

LEXIE: I'm nothing like you.

CAROLYN: You're exactly like me. Strong. Stubborn. Angry. Confused. Demented. Lonely. Terrified. We're just alike.

LEXIE: I'm not like you. If I thought I was like you I'd kill myself.

CAROLYN: You were my favorite. You were always the one I loved the most. But you always scared the hell out of me. Even before you could talk, you'd stare at me with those eyes of yours and I'd think, oh, God, she knows. She knows.

LEXIE: Knows what?

CAROLYN: I don't know.

(pause)

LEXIE: Well, if you're not going to kill me, then I suppose I might as well kill you.

CAROLYN: You're not going to kill me.

LEXIE: Why not?

CAROLYN: Because if you kill me, you'll be all alone.

LEXIE: I don't care.

CAROLYN: Yes you do.

LEXIE: I don't care what happens to me.

CAROLYN: You might think you don't care, but you're terrified of being alone.

LEXIE: How do you know?

CAROLYN: Because you're just like me.

(pause)

LEXIE: That's why you didn't kill me? Because you're afraid of being alone?

CAROLYN: Nothing in the world scares me more. Except being loved.

(pause)

LEXIE: Then I suppose if I want to really hurt you I should tell you I love you and then leave.

CAROLYN: I suppose you should.

(pause)

LEXIE: All right.

(Lexie stands up, looks at her. Picks up a baseball sized rock. Whacks Carolyn hard over the head once with it. Carolyn keels over, stunned, holding her head.)

LEXIE: I love you, Mother.

(Pause. She drops the rock.)

Goodbye.

(Lexie goes. Carolyn staggers to her feet, holding her head.)

CAROLYN: You'll be back. I know you'll be back. A mother knows.

(The light fades as she staggers into the house and up the steps.)

Find And Sign

Wendy MacLeod

Comic
Julia, thirties, smart, Bronx public high-school teacher
Mona, thirties, stunning, works for Vogue, British-y accent

*In their Upper West Side (NYC) studio apartment, roommates
Julia and Mona discuss Julia's one-sided flirtation with Iago
at a Tribeca loft party the previous night. Julia struggles to
understand Iago's indifference to her advances, choosing to
believe that he must have been put off by her simple appear-
ance and her emphasis on intelligence. Julia tempts compar-
ing Mona's captivating beauty to her own, but Mona defers
and tries to coax Julia into laying aside her pickiness and
take risks in order to find someone she could love.*

JULIA: He wasn't even that nice. So why was I working so
   hard?
MONA: Because he wasn't nice?
JULIA: Maybe he is. We don't know.
MONA: Did he seem nice?
JULIA: He seemed restless. Best case scenario, mildly
   amused.
MONA: Maybe he was intimidated by you.
JULIA: You always say that.
MONA: You're very quick, very verbal.
JULIA: So was he.
MONA: I get intimidated by you.
JULIA: I go out of my way to demonstrate my smartness, and
   it just puts people off.
MONA: Not people. Men.
JULIA: Ugh. Why do I do that?
MONA: *(British pronunciation)* You're supposed to ask them
   about themselves.
JULIA: I did. And what you just said is so 1950's.
   (Mona shrugs.)
We talked endlessly about him being called Iago . . .

MONA: Iago. How do I know that name?

JULIA: Shakespeare.

MONA: No, I met an Iago once . . .

JULIA: The point is. We talked endlessly about his weird name. Did he ask me a question? He did not.

MONA: So why did you give him your mobile?

JULIA: Uh, it's so humiliating. I gave him my number when he didn't even ask for my number. I gave him my number even though he was staring at some model the whole time!

MONA: Staring?

JULIA: Looking . . . .

MONA: Well darling they're gonna look . . .

JULIA: I mean, he wasn't rude . . .

MONA: Was he there with a date?

JULIA: He was there with his boss.

MONA: Well that's good.

JULIA: Then why hasn't he called?

MONA: Maybe he's involved with someone.

JULIA: He was being very cagey . . .

MONA: In which case it was perfect that you gave him your number because he couldn't ask.

JULIA: It's perfect unless he has a wife and three kids, in which case I'm a ho'.

MONA: Do you think maybe this guy is The One?

JULIA: Don't be retarded.

MONA: Why is that retarded?

JULIA: We met at a party. We were drinking grain alcohol punch. It wasn't like one of your bodice-rippers . . .

MONA: That was historical fiction. I learned a lot about the Tudors!

JULIA: You should read better books.

MONA: Why?

JULIA: Because your father is a writer.

MONA: I just read them for entertainment.

JULIA: They're not supposed to be entertainment! They're supposed to be books!

MONA: I read my father's books.

JULIA: You try to read your father's books . . .

MONA: Maybe he was gay.

JULIA: Why would he pretend to be straight?

MONA: Did he say he was straight?

JULIA: No, but when I suggested, you know, leaving together, he didn't tell me I was barking up the wrong tree.

MONA: You suggested leaving together?

(Julia shrugs.)

You are a ho'.

JULIA: I don't have much time. I have a limited number of eggs.

MONA: Do you even want children?

JULIA: Everybody wants children.

MONA: Not me.

JULIA: Romance is like a puzzle. You have to use your brain. You have to ask; how can I intrigue this person?

MONA: How did he intrigue you?

JULIA: By not giving a damn.

MONA: Well then, you do that.

JULIA: I can't.

MONA: If he didn't ask for your number, and he didn't leave when you suggested leaving . . .

JULIA: I know.

MONA: Men never say no to sex . . .

JULIA: I know.

MONA: Maybe he'd drunk too much and was worried about his performance!

JULIA: Or maybe he's on anti-depressants . . .

MONA: A lot of them are . . .

JULIA: And of course there's one other possibility.

MONA: Stop . . .

JULIA: That he didn't find me attractive.

MONA: But you are.

JULIA: No you are.

MONA: That doesn't mean you're not. Maybe . . .

JULIA: What?

MONA: He actually cared about you too much to just . . .

JULIA: Get real.

MONA: Look, there are a million fish in the sea.

JULIA: This is New York. There are like six.

MONA: Why don't you ring him?

JULIA: Do you ever have to call them?

MONA: I have.

JULIA: When?

(Mona struggles to think of a time.)

JULIA: What must that be like? To know that every man you meet wants you.

MONA: Every man I meet doesn't want me . . .

JULIA: What's the percentage would you say?

MONA: Anyway, why do men have to do the calling?

JULIA: Because they like it.

MONA: According to who?

JULIA: Whom. Cosmo. They're hunters and gatherers.

MONA: We are too. Look at lionesses. Do you know his last name?

(Julia nods.)

Then Google him. How many Iagos can there be in Manhattan?

JULIA: I'll look pathetic.

MONA: You'll look confident. Have an extra ticket to something.

JULIA: He'll see through that.

MONA: People have extra tickets all the time.

JULIA: So I have to buy two tickets and pretend I have an extra? That'll cost a fortune.

MONA: It's an investment.

JULIA: What if he says no? Then I'll really have an extra ticket.

MONA: I'll buy it from you.

JULIA: You don't even know what it's to!

MONA: You're just scared.

JULIA: He was . . . formidable in his way.

MONA: So are you.

JULIA: Am I?

MONA: You know you are.

JULIA: Except in this one area of my life . . .

MONA: You know what I do? When I'm too interested in a guy? I get interested in another guy. And then when I stop wanting the first guy, he starts to want me!

JULIA: But Mona, for that to work, you'd have to have two guys in play at any given time.

MONA: So?

JULIA: My problem is I have zero men in play.

MONA: Whatever happened to that Roger guy?

JULIA: He had dyslexia.

MONA: So you broke up with him?!

JULIA: I found his grocery list. My God. The spelling.

MONA: It's a learning disability!

JULIA: I know! But I couldn't have an orgasm after I saw that list.

MONA: But you're a teacher!

JULIA: Exactly. It was a busman's holiday.

MONA: I'm thinking maybe your standards are too high.

JULIA: Because I require literacy?

MONA: See if Iago has a friend. Say you're trying to fix me up.

Information on this playwright may be found at
www.smithandkraus.com. Click on the AUTHORS tab.

Home Of The Great Pecan

Stephen Bittrich

Comic
Tammie, late twenties
Rosy, mid-twenties

In the sleepy town of Seguin, Texas, whose biggest export is the pecan, Tammie Lynn Schneider is desperate to get married again. At the ripe age of twenty-nine in south Texas, she fears she's almost over the hill. For years, she's been working on her boyfriend, Greeley Green. The night before this scene, Greeley was to execute a romantic "surprise" proposal on the dance floor of the Corral, a popular two-step dance hall, but instead, since Greeley was short the necessary $2000 to buy her the engagement ring of her choice (and generally freaked out about marriage), he just didn't show up. Instead, while cruising around Seguin, he allowed himself to be seduced by the overly friendly 7-11 check-out girl, Wendy. Bad timing. "Nosy" Rosy walked in and caught him making out right between Pac Man and Altered Beast in the video game room. In this scene Tammie finds out from her best friend, Rosy Fay Stadtmueller, the local church mouse who is having a secret affair with the married minister, that Wendy isn't the only other woman Greeley's been stepping out with. The scene takes place on the back porch of Tammie Lynn's country home where the crickets and bullfrogs are annoyingly active.

TAMMIE: SHUT UP! JUST SHUT THE HELL UP!!! God-
    damned crickets! Goddamned crickets!
ROSY: Tammie Lynn!
TAMMY: What?
ROSY: Don't take the Lord's name in vain.
TAMMIE: Oh.
    (beat)
    Sorry, Lord.
    (Tammie sobs out loud.)
    That bitch! That damn video game harlot bitch!

ROSY: Now, now, Tammie. Don't let her get to ya. She ain't worth it.

TAMMIE: *(At first sentimental)*
Greeley . . . Greeley—
(Then—)
Dickless son-of-a-bitch!

ROSY: Tammie!

TAMMIE: Or he will be when I get a holt to him next.

ROSY: Well, if you ask me, he ain't worth it either.

TAMMIE: Well, I guess I ain't asked you.

ROSY: Some thanks.

TAMMIE: If you hadn'ta butt your nose inta Seven Eleven that late at night, none of this woulda happened.

ROSY: That's right. Shoot the messenger.

TAMMIE: Miss Nosy.

ROSY: *(after a beat)* I just do it for you. I hate to see how he hurts you.

TAMMIE: That's my business.

ROSY: I guess I'll jes' keep to myself next time.

TAMMIE: That'd be best.

ROSY: Just turn a blind eye every time he steps out on you.

TAMMIE: I'd prefer that.

ROSY: All right.
(pause)

TAMMIE: Whadda you mean "every time"?

ROSY: *(innocently)* What?

TAMMIE: Whadda you mean by sayin' "every time he steps out on you"?

ROSY: *(after a beat)* Nothing . . . or should I say "nada."

TAMMIE: Nada?

ROSY: That's Spanish for "nothing."

TAMMIE: I know what it's Spanish for, Rosy, my momma didn't raise no dumb ass. Why'd you say nada?

ROSY: No lo se.

TAMMIE: I'm about to kick yer butt.

ROSY: You said you didn't wanna know nada about nothing. Every time I open my mouth I just get chewed out. Why should I say anything at all?

TAMMIE: Puta! Pendejo!

ROSY: I know what that means, Tammie.

TAMMIE: You better spill the beans, Rosy Fay Stadtmueller.

ROSY: I heard Greeley was takin' Spanish lessons back in July.

TAMMIE: What?

ROSY: Yeah, from Cynthia Morales.

TAMMIE: When?

ROSY: They was seen together at the Oak. He was teachin' her how ta play pool, and she was teaching him how ta say it all in Mexican.

TAMMIE: Is that all?

ROSY: They say he had his arms all around her. Showin' her how ta hold the stick.

TAMMIE: Well, that don't mean—

ROSY: And they say she was drivin' around in his pickup truck.

TAMMIE: His truck!

ROSY: Well, thas' what I heard.

TAMMIE: Nobody drives that truck. He don't even let me drive that truck. Who tole you?

ROSY: I heard it from . . . I can't tell you, but it's true. I know it's true.

TAMMIE: Who from?

ROSY: Well . . . you can't say nothing.

TAMMIE: I ain't .

ROSY: Reverend Pat tole' me. Cuz Cynthia got baptized and born again. She tole' him, so you can't say nothing.

TAMMIE: That Mescun pool hall slut!

ROSY: They'd been drinkin' a course. Maybe even takin' that Spanish Fly.

TAMMIE: She's got big ole tamale eatin' hips!

ROSY: Now hon, watch what stones you throw. She has found Jesus Christ after all.

TAMMIE: Ain't too many men she hasn't found.

ROSY: Tammie! Don't talk that way! Christ is there for anybody who wants him.

TAMMIE: Who else has he been with? Who else!

ROSY: Yer startin' ta get too upset now.

TAMMIE: You know, I got a good mind ta jes' leave him—once and for all. Jes' take that bus on up ta New York City—

ROSY: Oh, now yer talkin' crazy.

TAMMIE: Jes' take a taxi cab right on over ta ABC Studios. I'd
wait out there all day long until Tad from All My Children
comes out—

ROSY: Oh my Lord—

TAMMIE: I'd walk right on up ta him and say: "Excuse me,
Tad, I'm Tammie Lynn Schneider from Seguin, Texas, and
I jes' traveled two thousand miles on a Greyhound bus ta
be yer love slave.

ROSY: Oh, you better get those thoughts right outta yer head!

TAMMIE: How could he refuse an offer like that?

ROSY: Tammie Lynn, you are almost married again. Yer this
close. And Greeley's not a bad catch—with a little cleanin'
up . . . and with a little help from Reverend Pat and the
Lord. Now's not the time ta be thinkin' about livin' in sin
in some Yankee Babylon.

TAMMIE: A lifetime of sin with Tad would be worth an eternity
of hell fire.

ROSY: Now stop that!

(beat)

You are losin' yer marbles. I'm gonna speak ta Reverend Pat
in yer behalf. I have some influence with him. He can talk
ta Greeley. He's got a real gift. I bet he could get Greeley
ta give up his ways.

TAMMIE: Oh, fat chance.

ROSY: You jes' leave it up ta me. All you gotta do is get Greeley
inta church tomorrow.

TAMMIE: Two Sundays in a row? I dragged him kickin' and
screamin' last week.

ROSY: You jes' get him there! This man is in peril! And for that
matter, so are you. You gotta devilish look in yer eye.

TAMMIE: I'm gonna get him where it hurts.

ROSY: Where's that?

TAMMIE: I don' know. Cut his balls off.

ROSY: Now that ain't very Christian-like.

TAMMIE: Put cyanide in his Lone Star.

ROSY: Maybe revenge ain't the best way, darlin'.

TAMMIE: Take a chainsaw to his pickup truck.

ROSY: Don't even think those thoughts—

TAMMIE: *(suddenly hit with an idea)* Oooh, that's jes' too
good.

ROSY: What?

TAMMIE: Yeah, that'll get 'im where he lives.

ROSY: Tammie, hon, are you all right?

TAMMIE: I know how I'm gonna get Greeley.

ROSY: You do?

TAMMIE: *(After a beat; "yep" is like Ed would say it)* Yep. I'm gonna seduce Ed.

Information on this playwright may be found at www.smihandkraus.com. Click on the AUTHORS tab.

I COULD NEVER LIVE HERE

C.S. Hanson

Dramatic
Kirsten, eighteen
Wendy, twenty-three half-native American, Kirsten's cousin

Kirsten and Wendy are in a farmhouse in the middle of North Dakota. Kirsten wants to leave and go home to the Twin Cities. She doesn't know that her parents have split up for good and her father returned to his native New York City. Last night, Wendy came to the farm to visit her own father, only to find out she arrived on the day of his funeral. Kirsten wants to leave. Wendy wants to stay. It is 1984.

KIRSTEN: Mom? Dad?
   (She looks out the door, then goes to the fridge and gets OJ, a loaf of bread and peanut butter, and brings it to the living room to eat. She holds up a letter. Wendy enters from outside.)
WENDY: Hey, that's my—
   (She gathers up the letters.)
KIRSTEN: Sorry. Really. Sorry. I didn't know. They were just sitting here. You can leave them.
WENDY: Doesn't matter.
KIRSTEN: It does—I'm really sorry.
WENDY: You say that a lot.
KIRSTEN: What?
WENDY: Sorry
KIRSTEN: Sorry. I mean—no, but I am. I thought maybe there was a note for me. From my mom and dad. Did they go to town? The car's gone . . . I slept so late.
WENDY: Where'd you get the cap?
KIRSTEN: Upstairs.
WENDY: Probably belonged to—
KIRSTEN: Oh. Yeah. Johnny. Sorry. I shouldn't have just—do you mind? I didn't know henna could be so extreme.
WENDY: If I were blonde, I'd keep it that way.
KIRSTEN: Dirty blonde. Boring, like every other girl in my class.

WENDY: What's so bad about that?

KIRSTEN: But I'm not like everyone else. I just look like it. That's why I do things, you know, to my hair. Besides, my dad's family is mixed up with Italian, Irish, even Russian. I'd love to look a little exotic. God, I need new product.

WENDY: I used to dye my hair.

KIRSTEN: But I love your hair. Leave the letters. I won't read them, I promise.

WENDY: I've been putting them in order, from the first letter he wrote me to the . . . last. Like that will do any good.

KIRSTEN: Bummer.

WENDY: "Love, Dad." That means something, right?

KIRSTEN: I guess. I mean, yeah. Sure it does.

WENDY: Is that how your dad signs his letters?

KIRSTEN: Um, my dad doesn't send me letters. We go everywhere together—I mean, vacations, the three of us. Last year Hawaii. I wish they'd get a move on.

WENDY: What was the funeral like?

KIRSTEN: You don't want to hear about Hawaii? We went in December, during my school break.

WENDY: Do I look anything like Johnny?

KIRSTEN: I sent a postcard to myself. "Dear Kirsten: Weather is beautiful. By the time you read this, you'll be back in Minnesota freezing your you-know-what off!"

WENDY: I know I don't look anything like Johnny.

KIRSTEN: Last time I saw Johnny, I must have been ten or eleven.

WENDY: You saw him in the coffin, didn't you? Less than twenty-four hours ago?

KIRSTEN: It was my first funeral. I'm sorry. I didn't look for very long. It gave me the heebie jeebies. Sorry. Really.

WENDY: What was the funeral like?

KIRSTEN: Gee, I'd love to talk, but they'll be back. And watch, it'll be like hysteria to get on the road again.

WENDY: Why don't you just tell me what it was like?

KIRSTEN: Okay, but, the only reason I agreed to go to the funeral—well, my mom made me—but part of me thought, the three of us, getting in the car, it's like a little vacation, where we leave our problems behind. We make 'em stay in the house—you know, the bills and my dad's office with all

the folders stacked to the ceiling, and my mom's lists, and
my violin and all the music I'm supposed to be practicing—
it all has to stay and we get to leave.

KIRSTEN (cont.): Hasn't been much of a vacation.

(She heads toward the stairs.)

WENDY: Your dad left.

KIRSTEN: They're in town, right?

WENDY: He took the car. He left. He's gone.

KIRSTEN: What do you mean?

WENDY: It was late—or, early—this morning. I heard him
leave, something about catching a flight. New York, maybe?
Your mom slept on the couch.

KIRSTEN: No way.

WENDY: I'm pretty sure.

KIRSTEN: He wouldn't.

WENDY: Sorry.

KIRSTEN: But he didn't say goodbye.

WENDY: Maybe he didn't know what to say.

KIRSTEN: This means . . . it's true. They're getting divorced.
I knew it. But I didn't know it. I should have known. I hate
this. Why didn't he . . . why didn't he . . . take me with?

WENDY: It's okay.

KIRSTEN: No it's not. It'll never gonna be okay.

WENDY: Your mom's coming back.

KIRSTEN: So what? She ruins everything.

WENDY: She seems okay.

KIRSTEN: Where is she anyway?

WENDY: She got that old pick-up started. Must have gone
into town.

KIRSTEN: I can't get stuck with her. It's so unfair. They must
have talked, you know, to figure out who gets to keep me.
Why did she have to win?

WENDY: Sometimes we don't get to choose. Your mom doesn't
seem so bad. Hey, she's my aunt.

KIRSTEN: Are you kidding? She expects things of me. She
thinks I'm some kind of great violinist. Okay, I'm good, really
good, but I don't want to play the violin the rest of my life.
I have these nightmares. I wake up right before I'm about to
stick my fingers in a cuisinart, and you know, the blades are
spinning at high speed. I wish I could talk to my dad.

WENDY: Call him.

KIRSTEN: You know what I want to do? I want to go to New York. I need to see him.

WENDY: That's a big trip.

KIRSTEN: I'm eighteen. I got my own AmEx for graduation. All I need is a ride to the airport.

WENDY: You sure about this?

KIRSTEN: I can charge anything, as long as I don't buy a car. Fargo's not that far. Do you mind?

WENDY: I hate to leave. What if your mother locks up the house?

KIRSTEN: I know you want to stay, but, my mom is probably selling this place right now.

WENDY: Can you sell a farm in one day?

KIRSTEN: My mom sinks her teeth in? She'll sell. You know why? To show my dad she can. I see everything. That's the way it is being an only child.

WENDY: I never felt like an only child, even though I was. I just felt like a half circle that wanted to be whole. I paint a lot of shapes that aren't complete.

KIRSTEN: Like some of Johnny's paintings?

WENDY: What was the funeral like?

KIRSTEN: My mom will tell you. I have to ask you something.

WENDY: What?

KIRSTEN: If you end up staying, what are you going to do here? I mean, there's nothing going on. They don't even have a mall.

WENDY: There's work to do. Gonna grow vegetables on that patch that's gone to weed. I'll sell carrots and radish and lettuce along the interstate. And maybe my own paintings.

KIRSTEN: You won't get lonely?

WENDY: You can be lonely with people around you.

KIRSTEN: The wrong people, you mean.

WENDY: Few months ago, my boyfriend left. Jerk. At first I was so mad, but then I was relieved. Coming here? It felt right. Still does. I'll find a way to stay. I am not leaving Dakota du Nord. Let your mom give you a ride to the airport, huh?

KIRSTEN: Um, if you give me a ride, I'll tell you about the funeral.

WENDY: That sounds like a bribe.

KIRSTEN: A what? No way, José. We're cousins.

WENDY: Been bargaining for things all my life. That's how it works. So why don't you tell me what the effing funeral was like? Because if you do, we'll take the Harley out for a spin.

KIRSTEN: Really? Okay, Wendy, I'll give you every detail I remember if you give me a lift. But I'm warning you: I remember everything. Because I'd never seen a dead person before. So I stared. And his face? It was full of these really deep wrinkles. Uncle Johnny never opened a jar of face cream, that's for sure. But he looked like someone who had things to say. It was sad, thinking he'll never talk again. And, you should know this: I think your father was handsome.

WENDY: Wow. That's really good.

KIRSTEN: I have a lot more to tell you.

WENDY: Good. Great. I want to hear more. I think I need a . . . Let's go into town. You can tell me all the rest over a drink.

KIRSTEN: A drink? Like in a bar? I need to get to the airport.

WENDY: Yeah, okay . . . Here's the thing: Bad luck to blow out of a town without . . . see, growing up, every town we stayed in, even for one night, before we'd leave, we'd have a drink and make a toast: "Happy Times Ten."

KIRSTEN: Is that an Indian ritual?

WENDY: Yeah . . . . No. My mom made it up. She said if something holds you up . . . you stay . . . and if not, you move on.

KIRSTEN: Nothing's going to hold me up in this place.

WENDY: Ever ridden passenger on a Harley?

KIRSTEN: I can't wait. I'll get my things.

Information on this playwright may be found at
www.smihandkraus.com. Click on the AUTHORS tab.

INSTINCT

Matthew Maguire

Dramatic
Lydia Makarova, thirties, biochemist and vaccinologist
Fermina Maria Santos, thirties, biochemist and vaccinologist

It's Day 7 of a SARS outbreak. Lydia and Fermina are scientists at the Centers for Disease Control. They have been working around the clock, and they are unraveling. They are a couple who have lived together for 16 years. Lydia's prescription addiction to Oxycontin is exacerbated by the stress of the epidemic they are fighting to contain. Under the surface is Lydia's jealousy of an affair Fermina had years ago with a man. Lydia has recently discovered Fermina flirting with their partner in the lab, Daniel, and that has reawakened the crisis, as has Fermina's questions about having a child.

FERMINA: It might be all night, so save your strength. Good news—after a week, the data's faster every day.

LYDIA: This waiting feels like Moscow. In Moscow seven days equal seven years.

FERMINA: So at one year a child is actually 365 years old.

LYDIA: Da. We are an old people. Vodka and yogurt save us from death.
    (pause)

FERMINA: Have you ever thought of having a child?

LYDIA: This is your idea of small talk to pass the time?

FERMINA: Have you?

LYDIA: Thought is infinite.

FERMINA: Have you?

LYDIA: *(snapping)* OF COURSE! Don't be ABSURD! It's like question, have you ever thought of killing yourself? Everyone's *thought* of it, but no one admits it!

FERMINA: Lydia! Calm down! I didn't mean to set off one of your daily shitstorms. I was just thinking—

LYDIA: *(mocking)* About your biological clock?

FERMINA: Aren't you aware of your body changing? Why are you being so nasty?

(In the ensuing argument they tumble over one another.)

LYDIA: We are fighting SARS epidemic at the same time—

FERMINA: And don't you think I'm on edge, too, for—

LYDIA: While we should be working—

FERMINA: Daniel's parents?

LYDIA: On PUBLISHING before Picconi gets there first!

FERMINA: You're so off base. I'm worried about you.

LYDIA: *(reaching for her pills)* I'll be fine. *(taking a pill)* Worry about publishing.

> *(pause)*

FERMINA: You know what the techies call that?

LYDIA: It's OxyContin. And I've got a prescription.

FERMINA: They call it Hillbilly Heroin.

LYDIA: If you had pain I do, you would not be up on your horse.

FERMINA: Pun intended?

LYDIA: What?—No! Stop it! It is absolutely legitimate.

FERMINA: Oh my god, your operation was successful, and your shoulder was healed a year ago!

LYDIA: Whose shoulder is it?

FERMINA: It's as strong as morphine.

LYDIA: Dr. Benson says I'm fine.

FERMINA: How many doctors do you have?

LYDIA: Are you accusing me?!

FERMINA: Are you doctor shopping?

LYDIA: You are fierce little researcher, are you not!

FERMINA: Lydia, it's a narcotic! Is Benson just stupid, or is he helping Big Pharma milk you?

LYDIA: You can go to hell!

FERMINA: Your denial's scaring me.

LYDIA: My medications are private!

FERMINA: We've lived together for sixteen years!

LYDIA: Even from you. I am warning you. Leave me alone.

FERMINA: I'm trying to help you—

LYDIA: Go away!

FERMINA: That's enough, we have to go home and sleep.

LYDIA: I just have a little more to do. Go ahead.

FERMINA: You first.

LYDIA: You don't trust me alone?

FERMINA: How many pills did you take tonight?

LYDIA: I don't count.

FERMINA: YOU DON'T COUNT?!

(Lydia collapses, shaking violently.)

LYDIA: Please, I can't stop shaking. I can't . . . stop . . .

(Fermina wraps Lydia in her arms.)

FERMINA: There, I got you . . . I got you . . . it's okay.

(Long pause. Lydia begins to recover.)

LYDIA: Can we let it go for now?

FERMINA: Yes . . . shhhhh . . .

LYDIA: Talk to me about something.

FERMINA: What?

LYDIA: Anything . . .

(Long pause. Fermina takes the basketball tickets from her pocket.)

FERMINA: Look what Daniel gave us.

LYDIA: What are those?

FERMINA: Tickets to the Hawks game.

LYDIA: What am I missing?

FERMINA: It's a gesture.

LYDIA: Of what?

FERMINA: (*defensive*) Hey! He gave us *two*.

LYDIA: Why is he giving you gifts?

FERMINA: He gave me a *pair* of tickets. He's not giving *me* gifts.

LYDIA: People dying of SARS and you go to basketball game?

FERMINA: No, I'm not. (*pause*) Are you jealous?

LYDIA: The quarantine is not working, and you ask me I am jealous?!

FERMINA: We can't go any faster; we have to wait for results.

LYDIA: So you have time to watch some testosterone ritual of giant men in short shorts running up and down with their dribblets thrusting their balls in a net?

FERMINA: I said I'm not going! He said it was just a gesture.

LYDIA: He is lying.

FERMINA: You're outrageous! That's what he told me.

LYDIA: Of course that is what he said. Don't pretend to be naïve.

FERMINA: I shouldn't have shown them to you.

LYDIA: Why are you asking me if I have thought about a
    child?!
FERMINA: He's got nothing to do with that!
LYDIA: All right! Enough!
    (long pause; she collects herself)
    How many new cases?
    (long pause)
FERMINA: One hundred and seventeen.

*Information on this playwright may be found at
www.smihandkraus.com. Click on the AUTHORS tab.*

Lovesick or Things That Don't Happen

Lia Romeo

Comic
Stacy and Susie, both twenties to thirties

> *(Lights up on Susie and Stacy, both 25. In matching brides-maids' dresses. Each with a glass of champagne.)*

STACY: I'm so glad Mandy's getting married.

SUSIE: Me too. And I'm so glad she's getting married to Chuck.

STACY: Me too. And I'm so glad we're her bridesmaids.

SUSIE: Me too.

STACY: Best friends from college, and now Mandy's getting married! And we're her bridesmaids!

SUSIE: I know! Cheers!

STACY: Cheers!

> *(They drink their champagne. Stacy refills their glasses.)*

STACY: I just can't believe Mandy's getting married!

SUSIE: I know. I never thought any of us would get married.

STACY: I know! Especially Mandy.

SUSIE: I know. I mean, her nose—

STACY: Not that there's anything wrong with her nose.

SUSIE: No. But it's hard to get married.

STACY: I know! I mean, look at us. We're not getting married.

SUSIE: No.

STACY: I mean, I wish I was getting married.

SUSIE: I wish *I* was getting married.

STACY: But we're not. And Mandy is.

> *(beat)*

Which is great!

SUSIE: Cheers!

STACY: Cheers!

> *(They drink again. Stacy refills their glasses.)*

STACY: And Chuck's such a nice guy.

SUSIE: I know. And it's hard to find a nice guy.

STACY: I know. I wish I could find a nice guy.

SUSIE: I wish *I* could find a nice guy.

STACY: But we can't. And Mandy could.

(beat)

Which is great!

SUSIE: Cheers!

STACY: Cheers!

(They drink again. Stacy refills their glasses.)

SUSIE: I fucked him.

STACY: Who?

SUSIE: Chuck. I fucked Chuck.

STACY: You did?

SUSIE: Yeah.

STACY: Before they met?

SUSIE: Um.

STACY: After they met?

SUSIE: Yeah.

STACY: Susie!

SUSIE: I know.

STACY: Why?

SUSIE: Cause he's such a nice guy. And it was like, why should Mandy get such a nice guy? Why should she get such a nice guy, who shaves every day and makes two hundred thousand dollars a year and flies her to Paris for the weekend, when all I can get is Trent who only has one eye!

STACY: Trent only has one eye?

SUSIE: Yeah, the other one's fake. But don't tell him I told you. He's really sensitive about it.

STACY: Okay.

(beat)

I fucked him too.

SUSIE: Chuck?

STACY: Yeah.

SUSIE: Stacy!

STACY: I know.

(beat)

He's really good in bed.

SUSIE: I know.

STACY: Cheers!

SUSIE: Cheers!

(They drink again. Stacy refills their glasses.)

SUSIE: I also killed her dog.

STACY: Mr. Puddles?

SUSIE: Yeah.

STACY: But I thought Mr. Puddles got run over by a car.

SUSIE: He did. But I was driving.

STACY: Oh.

SUSIE: Yeah. I was going over to Mandy's house one day and it was right after she and Chuck got engaged, actually, and she was showing off her big beautiful ring all over the place, and I didn't have a ring, even though Trent and I had been together two years and she and Chuck had only been together six months, and Mr. Puddles was outside, and you know how he'd always bark?

STACY: He'd *always* bark.

SUSIE: I know, so I was driving up and he started barking, and . . . I just drove over him. And then he stopped barking. And I drove away.

STACY: Mr. Puddles was pretty annoying.

SUSIE: I know.

(beat)

STACY: Well, cheers!

SUSIE: Cheers!

(They drink. Stacy refills their glasses.)

SUSIE: I also did one more thing.

STACY: Yeah?

SUSIE: I put arsenic in the wedding cake.

STACY: You did?

SUSIE: Yeah.

STACY: Were you going to tell me?

SUSIE: Yeah.

STACY: I was going to eat that wedding cake!

SUSIE: I really wanted to tell you—but you know, I was nervous. Cause you and Mandy and I are best friends, and I always thought you liked me better than Mandy, but what if you didn't?—what if you liked Mandy better?—and what if you told Mandy I put arsenic in her wedding cake, and she got really, really mad? But since you told me you fucked her fiancé—well, I figured it'd probably be okay.

STACY: I do like you better than Mandy.

SUSIE: I like you better than Mandy too.

STACY: I figured you did. Since you fucked her fiancé, killed her dog, *and* put arsenic in her wedding cake.

SUSIE: Yeah.
>(beat)
>How much arsenic do you think it takes to kill people?
>Probably a lot, right?

STACY: Probably.

SUSIE: Probably a lot more than I put in, right?

STACY: Probably.
>(beat)
>How much did you put in?

SUSIE: A lot.

STACY: Hmm.
>(beat)
>Well, cheers!

STACY: Cheers.
>(beat)
>I think it's going to be a really amazing wedding.

SUSIE: Yeah.
>(She smiles.)
>Me too.

Information on this playwright may be found at
www.smihandkraus.com. Click on the AUTHORS tab.

PONZI

Elaine Romero

Dramatic
Catherine, Early forties
Allison, Mid-thirties

> *Catherine, a rich heiress, has just invested her money with Allison's financial manager—a man named Jack. Catherine has agreed to mentor Allison in how to be a "proper Philanthropist" while simultaneously pursuing Allison's husband.*

CATHERINE: Thanks for all your hard work on this. Really impressive.

ALLISON: *(blushes)* Oh, thanks.
    Of course, I know you do this kind of thing all the time.

CATHERINE: Not all the time.

ALLISON: Yes, you do. *(joking)* Do-gooder.

CATHERINE: There are those who do much more.

ALLISON: I bet you're on a thousand boards. I'm just a newbie.

CATHERINE: You'll get the hang of it. We raised a lot tonight. It's going to make a difference to the museum. And when you see the measurable impact of your hard work, you'll be hooked.

ALLISON: I admire you. I guess you know that.
    (Allison smiles, drops her head. Catherine touches Allison's face.)

CATHERINE: I admire you, too.
    (Catherine kisses the side of Allison's face.)
    Allison breaks away. She's giddy from the success.

ALLISON: *(shifts the topic)* Too bad Jack had to leave early. I think he could have gotten even more pledges.

CATHERINE: *(impressed)* Jack is a genius. No wonder they gave him his own cable TV show.

ALLISON: Oh, and that show makes so much sense. I'm so not a finance person, but I understand that show. And the people he gets. Those ladies who look like they could be homeless, but they're not. They're secret rich heiresses who use newspaper instead of toilet paper because they're so CHEAP. I read about them in *Time* magazine. It was this article about these people who were so rich that they were totally *immobilized*. Such self-control.

CATHERINE: They're like the anorexics of money. No Prada for them.

(Allison laughs.)

ALLISON: And Jack got them to give. People who don't use real toilet paper. He's got a gift. A way of knowing how to read people, how to see the person inside the person inside the person. To look at someone and know what they're about. I want to be like that when I grow up. To look at someone in the face and know the absolute truth. To look someone in the face and know how far they'd go to get what they want.

(Catherine shifts. It's a bit awkward.)

CATHERINE: It's like my dad. I'd say good financial planners are all part psychologist if not parish priest. You're dealing with estates and families and drug addicted kids. Parents who want to disinherit their children and those who want to set them up for life. And the good financial planner pleases everybody. My dad used to say, from the sales point of view, you've got one task to "Find the need and fill it." And that's basically how you sell something and keep your customer happy. You sniff out the need and come up with your fancy solution. But first you've got to find the need. That deep deep need that a person hides from the rest of the world. And it's not insincere. Because you have taken care of the singular thing that is most important to that person. You listened and you heard what deep down inside really mattered.

(Allison thinks about it. She might be smarter than Catherine first thought.)

ALLISON: *(short pause)* What did I need? When I bought your tables.

Catherine puts her hands on Allison's shoulders.

CATHERINE: I'm not talking about us. I'm talking about them. I'm just saying that if I were a different person, I might enjoy sales. My dad always loved the thrill of the sale. He made money for fun. Because it gave him a rush. Because, in that moment, there was no one on earth that was more on the money than he was!

ALLISON: But I must have *needed* something. If your dad was right. And he was such an expert. On people. And sales.

CATHERINE: You didn't need anything. You were just being generous.

(Catherine touches Allison's arm, assuring her.)

ALLISON: Good, because I don't want to think I fell for something here. Catherine watches Allison, maybe trying to figure out what she knows. I don't want to be a chump.

CATHERINE: You are one of the few magnanimous people in the world.

ALLISON: I was being generous. I have a good heart.

CATHERINE: I was talking more about stockbrokers. Not us. Not people who are just trying to make sure the city they live in stays interesting and attracts good, new people. This is the kind of thing, this museum deal, which attracts good companies here. And they bring in more money. And cocktail guests. And interesting conversations. Art is what makes this place rich. Art is what makes us rich.

ALLISON: *(not sure)* Yeah. And I like what you say. How we're better because of this—museum. And how it makes our community more attractive. I like that.

CATHERINE: I've had a lot of years to think about it. I watched my mother and father serve on boards. It's kind of a family tradition. You work with people and you know that one has what the other wants, and you sort of agree to ignore that for the good of the community. I watched my parents dance that dance.

ALLISON: I watched my father watch football. I watched my mother do the dishes. I watched them retreat into that house. In the country. They never even went out to dinner. I remember the first time I went to a restaurant. As an adult. It was really odd. I walked into that place with my date, and I could hear the voices of all these people talking. The place was vibrating with politics and attitudes, and people were trying to talk louder than other people, so someone might overhear their conversations to see how important they were. And I just wanted to flee. Because I hadn't really been invited. I mean, my date had brought me there, but is that an invitation? I didn't belong there. I wasn't supposed to be in that building. I knew it. I wasn't like them. I didn't have whatever that restaurant wanted from its customers. Whatever made that restaurant bring in certain types of people. I didn't belong because I was supposed to be in a bubble. A quiet silent bubble and there weren't supposed to be people around me. I was supposed to be back in the country. With my parents. And our slutty dog. *(short beat)* She had five litters.

CATHERINE: The bubble. I've felt that way after returning from long trips abroad. Like English sounded assaulting to my ears. And the attitudes. Like "Why do you have such a heavy suitcase?" Because I was gone for six months and I went to over three continents. Like I owe an explanation to customs people. People who never even travel. I owe an explanation to them?

ALLISON: It's good you have all this experience. I need to learn from you. People still get pretty strange when I ask them for money. Like I'm a pickpocket. Bryce warned me but I wanted to be part of the community. I wish he could have come tonight. He got all agitated at the last minute. His head is always somewhere else.

CATHERINE: Well, next time. And we'll get you a place further up front. That mix up with you in the back was completely on me.

ALLISON: You'll help me, won't you? Teach me how to be a proper philanthropist?

CATHERINE: Absolutely.

ALLISON: You're so nice.

CATHERINE: I don't know.

ALLISON: No, you are—really. Out of the way nice.
(Catherine blushes.)
You're just humble.

CATHERINE: You know, I'm always reminded that I am where I am because of somebody else's efforts. That can be humbling.

ALLISON: I guess I'm in the same boat. I mean if Bryce didn't work so hard—

CATHERINE: It doesn't matter where it comes from. It's all

for a good cause. It's all part of the universal flow. And the museum will be pleased. And with another election coming up—

ALLISON: Oh, I don't even want to talk about another election.

CATHERINE: This country swings between hope and despair. I stay out of it.

ALLISON: But you vote—

CATHERINE: Every time. I'm a good citizen. Even when I'd lost total faith in the system because of the Supreme Court. Even when I'd decided there was voter fraud because of black box voting. It all comes down to the source code, you know. I still went to the ballot and cast my lot.

ALLISON: I'll probably vote this time.

(Catherine seems surprised but doesn't say anything.)

CATHERINE: Just vote your conscience. But we don't really talk about politics.

ALLISON: You just did.

CATHERINE: Oops. My bad.

(Allison waits, not sure about bringing it up. She picks up more stuff and takes her time.)

ALLISON: I got this weird call this morning. From some guy. Saying he was from some government agency. Had some questions about Jack.

CATHERINE: Which government agency?

ALLISON: I forgot to write it down.

CATHERINE: Did you get the first letter? Of the acronym? These things always come with acronyms.

ALLISON: No, I—

CATHERINE: What did he say?

ALLISON: Something about not saying anything to Jack. Right, I'm going to do that. Not say anything to Jack. I mean, I checked with him and he said not to worry. He said it was just some dumb thing from some paper work that got messed up. This was like five years ago. When Jack didn't even live here. It was just an old mess up. From the past. He knew exactly what that call was about.

CATHERINE: Um, well, what did the weird guy say exactly?

ALLISON: It's just normal. Par for the course.

CATHERINE: He said it was par for the course?

ALLISON: No, that was Jack. Par for the course. That's what Jack said. Par for the course. I don't play golf. That's from golf, right?

CATHERINE: The guy was from—you don't know the agency?

ALLISON: "E" something. "S" something. I don't know.

CATHERINE: You got a call from the SEC?

ALLISON: They just had some questions. About Jack.

CATHERINE: The Securities and Exchange Commission oversees people like Jack, Allison. They're like the money police. What kind of questions did they have?

ALLISON: Catherine, I don't know. He was really vague. He just said not to talk to Jack.

CATHERINE: But you did. You went straight to him.

ALLISON: I didn't really know what the guy was talking about.

CATHERINE: Did you ask the guy to explain? *(sarcastically)* Or, did you ask Jack to explain?

(Allison doesn't say anything, which seems to confirm Catherine's suspicion.)

ALLISON: Look, Jack has brought us something we never had.

CATHERINE: He has brought you something you never had. I already had it.

ALLISON: And he has made it. Have you seen his house? The government resents him because of his success. They hate people who find their way around the system.

CATHERINE: We need to find out what's going on. Now!

ALLISON: And these guys were acting like—they just don't know Jack. That is the thing I know for sure. They don't know Jack the way we do.

(Catherine starts stumbling around in her purse.)

CATHERINE: Damn. I left my phone at home. Presumably, they'd call me.

ALLISON: Catherine, it's okay.

CATHERINE: I have seen fraud, Allison. I can smell it from a mile away.

ALLISON: Then, we're okay.

CATHERINE: *(Trying to remain calm)* What did they say when you asked them to be more specific?

(Allison doesn't say anything. Catherine waits for Allison to explain.)

ALLISON: I hung up.

I hung up the call.

Jack's my Guardian Angel. Screw them.

CATHERINE: Did you get a name first? Before you hung up?

ALLISON: Screw them, Catherine, they don't know.

CATHERINE: What if they do?

ALLISON: Then, we'll deal with it.

CATHERINE: You told Jack.

ALLISON: Wouldn't you? *(beat)* Wouldn't you? It's the government. I know you vote, but do you really trust the government? The government.

(Catherine's silence seems to imply consent.)

It's going to be okay. You know fraud. You can smell it from a mile away.

CATHERINE: *(not so sure)* I can.

ALLISON: At least you have your cat.

Information on this playwright may be found at www.smihandkraus.com. Click on the AUTHORS tab.

Sex Curve

Merridith Allen

Comic
Marissa, twenty-seven to thirty-two, a biochemist
Robyn, twenty-seven to thirty-two, a sex-lit writer, Marissa's
roommate

> *Marissa's scientific experiment, which was meant to control
> who she falls in love with, has yielded some puzzling re-
> sults. Here, Marissa finds herself confused, exhausted, and
> questioning all that she has worked for. Robyn, Marissa's
> roommate, tries to encourage her to take the experiment in
> another direction.*

> *MARISSA looks as if she hasn't slept in days. She wears pa-
> jama pants, lab rat tee shirt and disheveled lab coat. When
> lights come up, Marissa is rummaging through the mess in
> her room. Looking for something. Anything that will help her
> figure out what's going on. In the midst of her research, she
> stumbles across a toy—it is the magic eight ball Josh gave
> to her. She picks up the eight ball, shakes it and slumps down
> next to her bed. She makes an 'ach' sound after looking at the
> results. Marissa crosses to her purse and fishes out a pack
> of cigarettes. She is about to light one but then quickly puts
> it down and darts for the magic 8 ball again. She shakes the
> toy harder, and then, looking at the results;*

MARISSA: Impossible!
   (A knock at the door.)
ROBYN (O.S.): Marissa? Do you want breakfast?
MARISSA: Not hungry.
ROBYN (O.S.): You skipped dinner last night.
MARISSA: Um . . . ok, maybe like, a muffin. And some cof-
   fee.
ROBYN (O.S.): I already made you coffee.
MARISSA: Well in that case . . .
   (She opens the door and picks up her cigarettes. She lights

up. ROBYN enters and sets down the coffee.)

ROBYN: What—Mar, are you stress smoking? Give me that!
(She takes the cigarette and puts it out.)

MARISSA: Oh come on.
(She tries to light another one and Robyn takes Marrisa's lighter.

MARISSA: Hey!

ROBYN: Drink your coffee.

MARISSA: Give me back my lighter.

ROBYN: I will not.

MARISSA: Robyn, I'm a grown woman and I want my lighter!

ROBYN: Forget it.
(Marissa tries to get the lighter back but Robyn throws it out the window.)

MARISSA: No you didn't!
(She takes a magnifying glass, holds it out the window with her cigarette.)

ROBYN: What the fuck do you think you're doing?
(Marissa expertly uses the sun to light her cigarette.)

ROBYN: Unbelievable.

MARISSA: Just like burning ants.

ROBYN: Fine, just—hold it out the window.

MARISSA: Fair enough.

ROBYN: Marissa, please talk to me.
(Beat as Marissa smokes.)

Look, I'm your best friend. It's not like I don't know what this is about. You're holed up in here stress smoking, all you want to eat is pastries and coffee, which I know is your break up, 'cause it's all I could get into you for days after Brian broke your heart in college. Except you haven't broken up with anyone and Lucas told me—

MARISSA: He told you? That bitch.

ROBYN: Is it true? Do you have feelings for the guy I think you have feelings for?

MARISSA: Honestly, I don't know what to believe! My biological impulses are going haywire. I'm not responding positively to sex with anyone anymore, I keep thinking about how much I don't want Josh to be involved with my research, but it doesn't make any sense. I'm not supposed to feel like this. I created that formula so this wouldn't happen.

ROBYN: You created the formula for a hormone released during sex—

MARISSA: I know. It's supposed to block the closeness urge, but, I don't know, what if this is a loophole? Can you really fall in love with someone you don't sleep with? I mean, really really?

ROBYN: Remember puberty?

MARISSA: Yes actually. I remember I used to have one of these too.

(She shows Robyn the 8 ball,)

ROBYN: You consulted a magic 8 ball before me?

MARISSA: I know! And you know what, all I keep getting when I ask it if I'm in love with Josh is "it is certain."

ROBYN: How many times did you do it—because you gotta figure it's a 50/50 shot—

MARISSA: *Every* time, which completely debunks every single probability theory I studied in undergrad. What does that mean?

ROBYN: Nothing, Mar. It's a fucking toy. But if you think it means something, maybe it's your subconscious telling you, you might be falling—

MARISSA: Oh my god . . . oh my god! What if the oxytosin blocker is completely bogus? What if—what if this loophole is the direct result of experimenting with that formula?

ROBYN: I was afraid something like this might happen. Mar, people aren't meant to be like that forever. It's like I first thought, if you're really in love maybe nothing can truly stop it.

MARISSA: If you're right my entire thesis is a failure.

ROBYN: But it isn't! Marissa, what if the whole sex curve serum is the same thing as a magic 8 ball? What if the serums is only real if you believe in it? And if that's the case, then nothing can truly stop love. Now answer me this; has anyone been able to offer some hard scientific proof that love isn't all biological and chemical?

MARISSA: Well…

ROBYN: Marissa it could be you! Talk to Josh—dare him to debunk your theory. Maybe you won't prove what you set out to prove, but what if you find out something else just as big?

MARISSA: No . . . no, it's too late. It's not that simple. There are so many factors to consider—

ROBYN: What's to consider? Come on, girl, you're in love!

MARISSA: No! I'm confused and tired and having a—an emotional response to my confusion. And besides even if it were true—this ridiculous notion that I could be, or should be in love with Josh, he's your ex, so I wouldn't even dream of going there.

ROBYN: Marissa, you know Josh and I were never soul mates—he's perfect for you—he's just like you—heady, brilliant, a little nuts—

MARISSA: I am not nuts! What I am is—maybe what's going on is that I'm having some sort of allergic reaction to this serum I've made.

ROBYN: You know that's not it.

MARISSA: No I don't! I don't know anything anymore. And that's exactly what I'm going to have to tell my thesis advisor. God, I'm dead. I'm gonna get kicked out of this program. I'll be a laughing stock.

ROBYN: Not if you take my damn advice!

MARISSA: Robyn, I love you, but you don't know what the hell you're talking about. Now please, leave me alone. You and Lucas, just leave me alone.

ROBYN: Marissa—

MARISSA: Get out! Just get out, please. Get out.

(Robyn hesitates but finally throws up her hands and exits. Marissa paces for a few beats, takes another cigarette, but realizes she still has no lighter and gives up. She flops down on the bed and pulls the covers over her head.)

THE TERRIBLE GIRLS

Jacqueline Goldfinger

Dramatic
Minnie: twenty-five years old, slow
Gretch: thirty years old, irreverent

Minnie has murdered Mr. Witherose and hidden his body because Mr. Witherose murdered his wife who was a mother-figure to Minnie. In this section, Minnie lies to Gretch about Mr. Witherose's death so that Gretch won't go looking for Mr. Witherose. Minnie also explains what happened on the day Mr. Witherose killed his wife, and why she feels partially responsible.

Minnie's alone in the dark lighting candles.In the background, we hear noise from the bar below—indistinguishable chatting, a football game, laughter.

(Minnie continues telling her story, in a whisper this time.)

MINNIE: And everything went good in the Darling House. Expect for maybe a cold here and a flu there. But it was all right. An' the boys grew up strong like their daddy, who liked their momma more for havin' them, an' they went to school in matchin' outfits, but everyone knew which was which from who was quiet and who was loud. An' she was lonely during the day when the boys were at school and so decided to open a restaurant, an' he said make it a bar. So she worked the days an' he worked the nights, an' each lived their dream in the same place that was diff'rent if the sun or moon was out.

GRETCH: (Off-stage:) Min, Minnie? Get on outta there! Come on, 'fore she sees you're missin' an' the door to the attic's open again.

MINNIE: (To candles:) Happy Anniversary. I'll be back
(Blows out candles and calls to Gretch)
Comin'!

(Gretch enters.)

GRETCH: She'll tan you good, you don't stop this.

MINNIE: But Mrs. Witherose was always good to me. An' I
    think she gets lonely up here.

GRETCH: If she's with God?

MINNIE: . . . then she's got all the comp'ny she needs.

GRETCH: An' if she's not?

MINNIE: Then she don't deserve no comp'ny.

GRETCH: Are you comparin' yourself to the Almighty?

MINNIE: No.

GRETCH: Then she's beyond needin' you for anythin', itnt
    she?

    (a pause)

GRETCH: Minnie?

MINNIE: She took me in when Momma kicked me out.

GRETCH: *(gently)* Come on now, let's go.

MINNIE: How'd you meet him, Gretch?

GRETCH: You know Minnie—

MINNIE: Please, Gretch?

GRETCH: I don't have time to be foolin' now.

MINNIE: Tell me, an' I'll come down, nice and quiet. I promise.
    Cross my heart and hope to die.

    (Gretch crosses her heart.)

GRETCH: Hope to die. Okay. One, only one, now. I didn't
    know her first, I knew him. Mr. Witherose put a call out in
    the local paper for girl waitresses. At the time I was dating
    Jimmy Hanson. An' Daddy'd thrown me out for one thing
    or the other, so I was at Jimmy's all the time. An' I came in
    to my interview with a big black eye. An' Mr. Witherose
    saw that an' hired me without any experience an' the next
    time Jimmy came to drop me off for work, Mr. Witherose
    was waitin' for him out back with a crowbar an' made a
    short order of that boy. Then he got me a place to live out
    in one a' his trailers by the river—

MINNIE: Where you still are today!

GRETCH: Yes, Ma'am. Now, let's get. Say goodbye now.

MINNIE: *(quietly)* Goodbye.

GRETCH: You think you can focus on the restaurant more,
maybe help out with more tables?

MINNIE: Why?

GRETCH: I was thinkin' of a vacation.

MINNIE: Disney?

GRETCH: No. Just a spend a little time on myself.

MINNIE: Where?

GRETCH: You can't tell Birdie, now.

> *(Minnie crosses her heart.)*

MINNIE: Promise. GRETCH: Atlanta.

> *(A beat)*

MINNIE: *(In a rush)* I lied to you this mornin'.

GRETCH: 'Bout what?

MINNIE: The call.

GRETCH: *(Grabs Minnie)* We got to go talk to Birdie, right now.

MINNIE: No . . . no . . . it's okay . . . it's just for you . . . after he asked . . . after y'all . . . he says . . . he says, "how's my Gretch doin'" . . . an' I say, "good, okay" . . . an' he was sayin', "I sure do miss her soemthin' awful" . . . an' I say, "yes, sir" and he says, "you be sure she's ready now," an' I say, "what does she need?" an' he says, "nothin', she's perfect just the way she is."

> *(Gretch beams.)*

I know Birdie's in love with him, an' I didn't wan' ta' hurt her feelin's none, so I didn't say word one before her. You won't tell her, will you?

GRETCH: Naw, I won't. Did he say, when he's comin' back? Last time he was here—

MINNIE: He was mad.

GRETCH: He was but . . .

MINNIE: He'd just as likely kill someone with that temper of his. So just stay here, okay?

GRETCH: But after, he said such wonderful things, Minnie, such wonderful things about our new life together.

MINNIE: Then why didn't he take you at the first?

GRETCH: There were complications.

MINNIE: Doesn't sound like no complications. Sound like, get in the damn truck an' lets go, woulda' done fine.

> *(Repeating what she'd heard)* Patience is a virtue.
>
> *(Looks Gretch in the eye)*

When he wants you, he'll come. We gotta take care a' one another 'til that happens. We're a family, at least a li'l bit.

You don' leave your folks, Gretch. That'd be just askin' for trouble. That's what Mrs. Witherose taught me. She said she's my folk, at least a li'l bit.

GRETCH: You don't understand.

MINNIE: I'm not stupid!

GRETCH: I'm not sayin' . . .

MINNIE: You don't say, but you an' Birdie think I don't know what's goin' on! You think I can't do nothin' 'cause I didn't go to school like y'all two! But I know things. Mrs. Witherose knew that I knew things. She knew I could do things, too!

GRETCH: Would you stop talk' 'bout her!

MINNIE: She was the first an' only that was every good to me!

GRETCH: We're good to you, Birdie and I!

MINNIE: 'Til you go an' jump after a chance, any chance, with that man, who wasn't much of a man anyways. You know what happens.

GRETCH: Nothin's gonna happen.

MINNIE: You know, you know, he hurt people he loves.

GRETCH Minnie!

MINNIE: You know those boys didn't mean no harm. You know Mrs. Witherose didn't mean nothin', an' she was, she was a good momma to those boys. She loved them an' she held them. He never did none of that, just roughhousin', made her so nervous, he was so big, an' they was both still such babies to her.

GRETCH: Minnie, there are people downstairs.

MINNIE: So when he got home an' saw the mess on the floor, saw the bits of his boys shot to pieces all ova' the floor, he came chargin' into the kitchen, an' he saw me there, an' he said "where's she at", an' I said, God forgive me in heaven to my dyin' day, I said, "at the restaurant." An' I shoulda' called right then, an' told her to run, but I didn't know he'd pick up the guns on the way out, taken 'em right outta' the boys cold little hands.

GRETCH: It wasn't your fault, she shoulda' been watchin' the boys, she knows you're not . . . experienced.

MINNIE: He left the guns out, after huntin' all afternoon, he left 'em out—

GRETCH: If she was watchin', as mother's are supposed to, an' isn't it her duty to—

MINNIE: I WAS WATCHIN' THEM. I was, I was watchin', I just, I's supposed to be, I just, just for a few minutes, while she took the biscuits ova', but then I went into the kitchen, it was just a minute, I swear, an' there were some loud bangs an' I got scared an' he came home an' I didn't call her to tell her . . . run! an' when I thought to call . . . no one answered . . . it just rang rang rang rang rang rang . . . it just . . .

(Gretch cradles her. They rock.)

GRETCH: I ain't her. I won't make the same mistakes.

MINNIE: He was the mistake, Gretch.

GRETCH: You don't understand.

MINNIE: 'Cause I'm stupid, huh? Then how come he calls when he knows you ain't here? He calls on the Minnie shifts.

GRETCH: I have—

MINNIE: Neither of y'all, he always calls when I work, don't he? You think that happens all by itself?

GRETCH: Maybe! Just maybe, sometimes, just maybe, you stupid cow! You just don't know what it's like to have someone love you so much you could just explode thinkin' 'bout it.

MINNIE: Neither do you!

Information on this playwright may be found at www.smihandkraus.com. Click on the AUTHORS tab.

Rights & Permissions

Monologues

4000 MILES © 2012 by Amy Herzog. Published by Theatre Communications Group in *After the Revolution and 4000 Miles*. Reprinted by permission of Theatre Communications Group. For performance rights, contact Dramatists Play Service, 440 Park Ave. S., New York, NY 10016 (www.dramatists.com, 212-683-8960)

ADORATION OF THE OLD WOMAN © 2010 by José Rivera. Reprinted by permission of José Rivera. For performance rights, contact Broadway Play Publishing, 224 E. 62nd St., New York NY 10065-8201 (www.broadwayplaypubl.com, 212-772-8334)

AFTER © 2011 by Chad Beckim. Reprinted by permission of Mark Armstrong, Paradigm Agency. For performance rights, contact Chad Beckim (chadbeckim1@yahoo.com). The entire text is published by Smith and Kraus, Inc. in *New Playwrights: The Best Plays of 2012* (www.smithandkraus.com).

AL'S BUSINESS CARDS © 2009 by Josh Koenigsberg. Reprinted by permission of Corinne Hayoun, Creative Artists Agency. For performance rights, contact Corinne Hayoun (chayoun@caa.com)

AN ACCIDENT © 2010 by Lydia Stryk. Reprinted by permission of Lydia Stryk. For performance rights, contact Broadway Play Publishing, 224 E. 62nd St., New York NY 10065-8201(www.broadwayplaypubl.com) 212-772-8334.

AMERICAN DUET © 2011 by Mark Leib. Reprinted by permission of Mark Leib. For performance rights, contact Mark Leib (meleib1@verizon.net).

AMERICAN LULLABY © 2010 by Cassandra Lewis. Reprinted by permission of Cassandra Lewis. For performance rights, contact Cassandra Lewis (casslewis@gmail.com)

AM I BLACK ENOUGH YET? © 2002 by Clinton A. Johnston. Reprinted by permission of Clinton A. Johnston. For performance rights, contact Clinton A. Johnston (caj@clintonjohnston.com)

ANY DAY NOW © 2009 by Nat Cassidy. Reprinted by permission of Nat Cassidy. For performance rights, contact Susan Schulman (schulman@aol.com)

BECHNYA © 2011 by Saviana Stanescu. Reprinted by permission of Saviana Stanescu. For performance rights, contact Elaine Devlin (edevlinlit@aol.com)

BLAME IT ON BECKETT © 2011 by John Morogiello. Reprinted by permission of John Morogiello. For performance rights, Samuel French, Inc. (www.samuelfrench.com, 212-206-8990)

CALL ME WALDO © 2011 by Rob Ackerman. Reprinted by permission of Peter Hagan, Abrams Artists Agency. For performance rights, contact Dramatists Play Service, 440 Park Ave. S, New York, NY 10016 (www.dramatists.com, 212-683-8960)

CARNIVAL ROUND THE CENTRAL FIGURE © 2011 by Diana Amsterdam. Reprinted by permission of Jonathan Mills, Paradigm Agency. For performance rights, contact Broadway Play Publishing, 224 E. 62nd St., New York NY 10065-8201 (www.broadwayplaypubl.com, 212-772-8334)

SCENES

3 TO A SESSION: A MONSTER'S TALE © 2005 by Desi Moreno-Penson. Reprinted by permission of Bruce Ostler, Bret Adams Ltd. For performance rights, contact Broadway Play Publishing, 224 E. 62nd St New York, NY 10065 (www. broadwayplaypubl.com, 212-772-8334)

… AND LA IS BURNING © 2010 by Y York. Reprinted by permission of Mark Orsini, Bret Adams Ltd. For performance rights, contact Broadway Play Publishing, 224 E. 62nd St., New York NY 10065-8201 (www.broadwayplaypubl.com, 212-772-8334)

BLOOD AND GIFTS © 2010 by JT Rogers. Reprinted by permission of Victoria Fox, Faber and Faber, Inc., an affiliate of Farrar, Straus & Giroux, LLC. For performance rights, contact Dramatists Play Service, 440 Park Ave. S, New York, NY 10016 (www.dramatists.com, 212-683-8960).

CALL ME WALDO © 2011 by Rob Ackerman. Reprinted by permission of Peter Hagan, Abrams Artists Agency. For performance rights, contact Dramatists Play Service, 440 Park Ave. S, New York, NY 10016 (www.dramatists.com, 212-683-8960)

CQ/CX © 2011 by Gabe McKinley. Reprinted by permission of Mark Armstrong, Paradigm Agency. For performance rights, contact Mark Armstrong (marmstrong@ paradigmagency.com) The entire text is contained in New Playwrights: The Best Plays of 2012, published by Smith and Kraus, Inc. (www.smithandkraus.com)

DARK PART OF THE FOREST © 2006 by Tammy Ryan. Reprinted by permission of Susan Gurman. For performance rights, contact Broadway Play Publishing, 224 E. 62nd St., New York NY 10065-8201 (www.broadwayplaypubl.com, 212-772-8334)

.